THE CELTIC REVIVAL IN
ENGLISH LITERATURE

The Bard

The Celtic Revival in English Literature

1760–1800

BY

EDWARD D. SNYDER

B.A. (Yale), Ph.D. (Harvard)

GLOUCESTER, MASS.

PETER SMITH

1965

16832

PREFACE

THE wholesome tendency of modern scholarship to stop attempting a definition of *romanticism* and to turn instead to an intimate study of the pre-romantic poets, has led me to publish this volume, on which I have been intermittently engaged for several years. In selecting the approximate dates 1760 and 1800 for the limits, I have been more arbitrary in the later than in the earlier. The year 1760 has been selected because it marks, roughly speaking, the beginning of the Celtic Revival; whereas 1800, the end of the century, is little more than a convenient place for breaking off a history that might have been continued, and may yet be continued, down to the present day.

Even as the volume has been going through the press, I have found many new items from various obscure sources, and I am more than ever impressed with the fact that a collection of this sort can never be complete. I have made an effort, nevertheless, to show in detail what has been hastily sketched in countless histories of literature — the nature and extent of the Celtic Revival in the late eighteenth century.

Most of the material here presented is now published for the first time. The chapter on Gray and Mason, however, is reprinted (with some additions) by kind permission of the editors of *Modern Philology*; and many of the essential facts were set forth in my unpublished dissertation at Harvard University in 1913.

I am glad of this opportunity of expressing my thanks to all those friends who have called my attention to various manifestations of the Celtic spirit that might have escaped my observation. My debt of gratitude is especially great to Professor Fred Norris Robinson and Professor Frank Edgar Farley; Professor George Lyman Kittredge and Professor Tom Peete Cross have likewise placed me under a heavy but pleasant obligation. Special courtesies extended in the libraries at Harvard, Yale, Cambridge, and the British Museum have greatly facilitated the work of collecting information about minor poets and dramatists; and my researches in the National Library of Wales at Aberystwyth were made effective through the kindness of John Ballinger, Esq., Librarian, Professor J. H. Davies, and Professor T. Gwynn Jones. Invaluable assistance in reading the proof has been given me by two of my colleagues at Haverford College, Professor John Alexander Kelly and Professor L. Arnold Post.

CONTENTS

ILLUSTRATIONS

THE CELTIC REVIVAL IN
ENGLISH LITERATURE

CHAPTER I

Introduction

I

THE DATE AND ORIGIN OF THE CELTIC REVIVAL

THE Celtic Revival with which we are concerned began about the year 1750. Like other great literary movements, it sprang from various remote sources which show a tendency in common; but as a movement in which any considerable number of people were interested it took shape in the middle of the eighteenth century.

Prior to that time a few distinguished scholars had shown considerable interest in the life of the ancient Celts — in their history, language, literature, customs, and in the ceremonies of their priests, the Druids. Individual historians, archæologists, and antiquaries had at odd times published weighty treatises on almost every conceivable feature of Celtic culture. Some of these, like John David Rhys's Grammar [1] (1592), were still regarded as authorita-

---

[1] *Cambrobrytannicae Cymraecaeve Linguae institutiones et rudimenta accuratè, & (quantum fieri potuit) succinctè & compendiosè conscripta*

tive in the eighteenth century. Others, more ephemeral, did little but arouse a temporary controversial interest and pave the way for subsequent works of a more substantial nature. To the archæologists one of the most interesting points of dispute was the origin of the numerous megalithic monuments of Britain — whether, in a word, Stonehenge and similar remains were built by Druids or not. This question was already of interest in the time of Nennius, and the twentieth century finds it still unsettled.[1] The linguists did creditably in compiling dictionaries of Irish, Gaelic, Welsh, and the minor Celtic dialects, and there were some ludicrous attempts to establish a close relationship between Welsh and Hebrew. Furthermore, whoever wrote a history of the early Britons was sure to include a few pages at least on Druidism.

Serious as these early scholars were in their Celtic researches, their enthusiasm was not shared by the general public. And amazing as is the list of technical monographs published before 1750, we cannot say that there was any great influence on English poetry and the drama. Here and there we find, to be sure, sporadic traces: Beaumont and

(London, 1592). This learned treatise was largely used by subsequent Celtic scholars and was not without influence on Thomas Gray. (See below, pp. 35–36.)

[1] For a bibliography of the books and pamphlets on Stonehenge, see W. Jerome Harrison in *The Wiltshire Archæological and Natural History Magazine*, December, 1901.

Fletcher introduced some Druidical elements into
Bonduca, and Milton made a passing reference in
Lycidas.

> Where were ye, Nymphs, when the remorseless deep
> Closed o'er the head of your loved Lycidas?
> For neither were ye playing on the steep
> Where your old bards, the famous Druids, lie,
> Nor on the shaggy top of Mona high,
> Nor yet where Deva spreads her wizard stream.

Dryden's *Masque of King Arthur* is also to be noted,
and there are a few other minor references.[1] Such tri-

---

[1] In turning the pages of several hundred eighteenth-century folios,
I have come across not quite a dozen pertinent passages written before 1760. Most of these are only incidental references, with no elab-
oration or description. In William Diaper's *Dryades; or the Nymphs
Prophecy* (London, 1713) Druids are twice mentioned (pp. 15 and 32),
but there is no evidence that the author knew a Druid from a Dryad.
In Welstead's *Oikographia* (London, 1725), an appeal for wine to
stock his new cellar, the poet casually refers to himself as a Druid.
With this may be compared the unimportant references on p. 11 of
the anonymous *Free Thoughts upon Faith* (London, 1746). More
significant is Thomas Cooke's short poetical romance, *The Bath* (London, 1726). The scene is laid in the time of King Cingetorix, and an
atmosphere of mystery is given by the reference to Druidism (pp. 6–
7). The poem also furnishes an example of the confusion of Celtic
and Scandinavian. (See below, pp. 9 ff.) Anticipating the spirit of
later Celtic forgeries comes the anonymous *Longford's Glyn; A True
History, Faithfully Translated from the Irish Original* (London, 1732),
replete with the spirit of classical mythology, faintly disguised as Celtic. At least it shows that Macpherson was not the first of his kind.
There are also a few poems in which "Contemplation" or "The
British Muse" is personified and represented as cherished by the
Druids. See Thomas Warton's *Pleasure of Melancholy* (written in
1745 and published anonymously in 1747) and William Whitehead's

fling symptoms as these are not, however, important enough to constitute a distinct literary movement. Throughout the seventeenth century and the first half of the eighteenth, there were no English poems of importance translated from Irish, Gaelic, or Welsh, and only a very few in which the mythology of the Druids played a serious part.

But the Celtic Revival was something definite; it was a real movement among English men of letters who were united by a common desire to infuse into English poetry the mythology, the history, and the literary treasures of the ancient Celts. And for the beginning of this Celtic Revival we naturally take that date when Gray's *Bard*, Mason's *Caractacus*, Macpherson's *Ossian*, and Evans's *Specimens of the Poetry of the Antient Welsh Bards* were generally understood and appreciated — that is, the years shortly after the middle of the century.

That the movement developed at just this time seems due to two chief causes, which, combining, made the seed take root, survive a short period of frosty satire and criticism, and blossom forth into a flower of acknowledged beauty. One of these causes was, of course, the awakening of the spirit of Romanticism. Special emphasis must, however, be laid

Verses to the People of England (London, 1758). Between these two dates there appeared an anonymous *Ode to Pleasure* (London, 1754), in which faint Celtic traces may be found. Jerome Stone's letter to the *Scots Magazine* on Gaelic poetry is quoted below, pp. 71 ff.

on one feature of the Romantic Movement, the desire to find a satisfactory substitute for the over-worked mythology of Greece and Rome. The contempt for classical mythology was becoming fairly common by the middle of the eighteenth century; and yet "for the production of a certain kind of sensational effect, some sort of supernatural 'machinery' was felt to be essential."[1] In order to satisfy this craving for "strangeness added to beauty" (which to Pater and others is the spirit of Romanticism), the poets were forced to abandon their familiar classical fields, and divert their attention to regions hitherto unexplored.[2] So it came about that shortly before the Scandinavian Revival set in,[3] English poets were already searching for facts about the rites and beliefs of the ancient Druids. As a substitute for Venus, Jupiter, Mars,

---

[1] For a discussion of this matter and the appeal of Norse mythology to the romantic poets, see F. E. Farley's *Scandinavian Influences*, p. 222.

[2] Gray wrote to Mason in praise of a passage in *Caractacus*; "Of all things I like your idea of 'the sober sisters, as they meet and whisper with their ebon and golden rods on the top of Snowdon'; and the more because it seems like a new mythology peculiar to the Druid superstition, and not borrowed of the Greeks." (*Letters*, ed. Tovey, I, p. 337.)

[3] "The earliest work in the English language intended primarily to arouse popular interest in Norse literature appears to have been a little meagre book whose title page reads; *Five Pieces of Runic Poetry Translated from the Islandic Language*." (Farley, *op. cit.*, p. 29.) This famous tract by Bishop Percy was drawn up for the press in 1761, and published in 1763.

and all the gods, demigods, and heroes with whom they and their readers were so familiar, they found a new set of figures — Hesus, Teutates, Andraste, and many others, whose names were yet unsullied by the vulgar touch. And though there was no Celtic pantheon so perfectly organized as that of Greece and Rome, nevertheless there were deities enough to furnish 'supernatural machinery.' There were, moreover, Druids, Bards, and Vates, whose human sacrifices and huge uncovered temples would give an effect truly awe-inspiring; there were heroes and heroines like Caractacus, Arviragus, Boadicea, Cuchullin, and Ossian, whose history was so curiously blended with fable as to be interesting beyond all measure.

Now as I have said, there always had been an undercurrent of Celtic study among British scholars. But just when the Romantic Movement was beginning to be felt in England, there arose by a peculiar coincidence, a Welsh antiquary and poet who was able to gather around him a large group of *literati* and to inspire them with a new zeal for Celtic research. Literary societies were founded, struggling translators were encouraged, and a tremendous mass of the lost poetry of the Welsh Bards was brought to light and published in Welsh and English. Needless to say, the genius to whom I refer was Lewis Morris, known to the Welsh as Llewelyn Ddu o Fon, a leading poet; known to such Englishmen as Bishop

Percy, Gray, and Mason, as the chief Celtic authority of the day. In the next chapter we shall consider his work and his influence on English literature.

The two primary causes, then, that combined to produce a real Celtic Revival were these: first, there was a newly awakened spirit of revolt, a desire to abandon the traditional classical mythology for something more romantic and mysterious; second, there was at this very time, a Welsh scholar who succeeded in unearthing certain treasures of Welsh literature that for centuries had been buried in obscurity. And the interest aroused by his discoveries was so great that not even the most trifling of English poetasters could afford to overlook them.

II

THE IGNORANCE OF DRUIDISM IN THE EIGHTEENTH CENTURY

Although recent studies by such well-informed scholars as Alexander Bertrand, Salomon Reinach, and Sir John Rhys have brought to light a vast amount of accurate information about the Druids, — information gathered from recently discovered monuments and documents of unquestioned antiquity, — the literary man of the mid-eighteenth century had surprisingly little knowledge of the subject. When there was hardly a native English scholar capable of reading Welsh, Gaelic, or Irish, and when so learned a man as Dr. Johnson could confidently deny the very existence of early Celtic MSS.,[1] the average poet had to rely on the accounts given by such classical historians as Cæsar, Tacitus, and Mela. While these accounts had been collected and printed by the antiquaries and historians, it was observed that they were frequently contradictory, and that when they did agree, they offered at best only a Roman interpretation of the Celtic religion.[2] Even the names of the Celtic gods had in most cases been transformed into the names of the Latin divinities that seemed to offer the closest parallel. What the average intellectual Englishman of 1750 knew about Druidism was presumably limited to the rudimentary facts set forth in the following paragraph.

There were three orders of Druids — the Druids proper, the Bards, and the Vates. By the time of Julius Cæsar they had become the ruling class in both Britain and Gaul, their highly organized corporation being presided over by an Arch-Druid of

[1] See *A Trip to the Western Islands of Scotland* (*Works*, 1787, X, p. 459), and the letter to Boswell of February 7, 1775, quoted in Boswell's *Life of Johnson*.

[2] For early protests against this *interpretatio Romana*, see Duclaux' *Discours sur la nature et les dogmes de la religion Gauloise* (Paris, 1769), p. xxxi, and Edward Ledwich's *Dissertation on the Religion of the Druids* (1785).

great influence. They worshipped certain gods and goddesses, taught the doctrine of metempsychosis or rebirth, and held both oak and mistletoe sacred. It is thought that they practised human sacrifice, and that they made use in their ceremonies of huge stone monuments which are still to be seen throughout Britain. In the Middle Ages there were numerous Welsh Bards (said to have been exterminated by Edward I), who may conceivably have been the descendants of the ancient Bards of pre-Christian days.

Knowing as we do to-day that Druidism was at its height several centuries before the Christian era, we cannot but wonder that the eighteenth-century critics were forever confusing the Druidism of the Celts with the Valhalla belief of the Scandinavians — a religion which dates from the days of the Vikings! But that they did confuse the two is undeniable. Professor Farley, who has made a detailed study of the matter, has already pointed out that Mallet, following Cluverius and Pelloutier, made the blunder in his *Histoire de Danemarc* but was corrected by Bishop Percy; that Mason did the same thing in *Caractacus;* that Gibbon called the Edda "the sacred book of the ancient Celts"; that for this same blunder the *Critical Review* attacked J. P. Andrews's *History of the Great Britain,* Joseph Sterling's ode *Scalder,* Charles Pougin's *Essai sur les Antiquités du Nord,* and an anonymous poem called

The Vision, though the *Critical Review* had itself
been guilty of the same offense in 1784, as had the
Monthly Review in 1775; and that the same general
mistake was made in Chatterton's *Battle of Hastings*,
Bowles's *St. Michael's Mount*, Sayers's *Moina*, and
in one of John Leyden's notes to his *Ode on Scottish
Scenery and Manners*.

In order to emphasize the frequency with which
this confusion between Norse and Celtic arose in
the eighteenth century, I venture to point out a
few other cases, of which Professor Farley has made
no mention. In 1761 there appeared in the *Annual
Register*, pp. 236–237, an English prose translation
of *The Incantation of Hervor* with the palpably absurd title "Fragments of Celtic Poetry, from Olaus
Verelius, a German writer; literally translated." A
few years later Pierre Chiniac de la Bastide Duclaux
spoke of "les Germains qui suivoient la Religion
des Gaulois leur Ayeux." [1] Again Richard Polwhele
in his *Fate of Llewelyn; or, the Druid's Sacrifice* in-
congruously introduced the "Fatal Sisters" in a
distinctly Celtic setting; and Jerningham apparently confused Norse and Celtic imagery in his *Rise
and Progress of Scandinavian Poetry*. In 1793 Joseph
Jefferson implied that Druids were priests of Thor
and Woden, and made the matter worse in an ambiguous note. Equally amusing is George-Monck

[1] In his *Discours sur la nature et les dogmes de la religion Gauloise*
(Paris, 1769), p. 60.

Berkeley's *Maids of Morven*, in which, by a strange oversight, the hero and heroine are transported to "Odin's hall." But the worst offender of all was John Joshua Proby, whose *Revenge of Guendolen* (1785) confused the Scandinavian, the Celtic, and the classical mythologies on a scale that is truly magnificent.[1]

To make matters still worse, when, towards the end of the century, there finally did come to be a general interest in Celtic antiquities, the leading authorities divided themselves into two opposing camps. On the one side were the "Celtomaniacs" — those wildly enthusiastic supporters of the Celtic cause whose creed a recent scholar has described so admirably:

La Celtomanie est une doctrine qui peut se résumer ainsi: "Les Celtes sont le plus ancien peuple de la terre; leur langue, mère des autres langues, s'est conservée presque intact dans le bas-breton; ils étaient de profonds philosophes, dont les révélations se sont transmises aux écoles bardiques du pays de Galles; les dolmens sont les autels où leurs prêtres, les Druides, offraient des sacrifices humains; les alignements sont leurs observatoires astronomiques."[2]

[1] See also above, p. 3, n. 1, for Thomas Cooke's blunder.
[2] Salomon Reinach in the *Revue Celtique* for 1898, p. 111. Among the worst of the Celtomaniacs were Pezron, Pelloutier, Aubrey, Stukeley, R. Colt Hoare, Latour d'Auvergne, Cambry, Edward Williams, and H. Martin.

A special type of the Celtomaniacs were the neo-Druids, who revived the cult of the ancient and mediæval Welsh Bards in a sentimental way, attributing to them various Christian doctrines of which they were probably ignorant.[1] On the other side were the anti-Celtic satirists,[2] insisting that any attempt to retrieve the lost literature of the Celts was inherently absurd, because "they are savages, have been savages since the world began, and will be forever savages while a separate people." Between these two adverse parties of scholars the average poet, and *a fortiori* the average reader, was in a bad way. Little enough was accessible about the Celts; that little was seriously confused with vague lore about the Scandinavians; and now this controversy was almost too much. Nevertheless, the poets went on writing Celtic-English poetry, and the public went on reading, more intelligently each year.

[1] For a detailed study, see Algernon Herbert's *Essay on the Neo-druidic Heresy in Britannia* (London, 1838). Contrast *The Welsh Question and Druidism* by "Griffith" (3d ed., London, 1888).

[2] For a collection of English satires against the Celts, with critical observations, see my article, "The Wild Irish," in *Modern Philology* for April, 1920.

III

THE TYPES OF CELTIC-ENGLISH POETRY
AND THEIR DEVELOPMENT

Perhaps the most convenient term for the poetry of the Celtic Revival, since it derived its inspiration from Celtic sources but was written in English, is "Celtic-English poetry." As we study its development in the latter half of the eighteenth century, it will be found to consist of four distinct types,[1] which appeared almost simultaneously and were frequently blended. It is possible, accordingly, to distinguish (1) poems dealing primarily with Druidism and other features of Celtic mythology, (2) poems translated from Irish, Welsh, or Gaelic, (3) imitations of these, or pretended translations, and (4) poems dealing with the famous heroes of Celtic history and tradition. But just as an arbitrary division of writing into exposition, argument, description, and narrative requires an immediate explanation that all four types of composition are frequently found in a single essay, so the division of Celtic-English poetry into these easily recognizable classifications necessitates an explanation that they

[1] The division I have made excludes, I fear too arbitrarily, the great mass of excellent poetry written in the Scottish dialect by Burns and others, yet the limitation of space have made such an exclusion imperative.

were frequently mingled to advantage in a single poem. Mason, for instance, based his dramatic poem *Caractacus* on early Celtic history with a great deal of Druidism intermixed; Macpherson translated from Gaelic about one seventh of his *Ossian* and pretended to translate the rest, while Sotheby added to his historical drama *The Cambrian Hero* numerous choruses written in imitation of the songs of the mediæval Welsh Bards.

Now the fourfold classification of this poetry, while of little critical value in itself, may suggest that the ignorance of Druidism was not so serious an impediment as might have been expected to the development of the Celtic Revival. A poet who knew little, and perhaps cared less, about the ceremonies of the Druids could write any of the three other types with reasonable assurance of finding an interested public. Similarly, readers who had no curiosity about Druidism might grow enthusiastic over Gray's renderings of the *Gododin*, Macpherson's *Ossian*, or any of the historical plays. Nevertheless, when a knowledge of Druidism became fairly general, the scope of this poetry was considerably enlarged.

It is evident, then, that a certain amount of antiquarian research on Druidism and a good deal of translation from Celtic were necessary before the Celtic Revival could reach its full development. A glance at the later chapters of this volume shows

that an important treatise dealing with Celtic mythology was printed practically every year from
1760 to 1800. Such a flood of information, while
doubtless to some extent a result of the poetry already published, was in turn a cause for the production of more poetry as fast as the public was able to
understand and appreciate it. Furthermore, many
of the poems and plays, like Llwyd's *Beaumaris Bay*
and Sayers's *Dramatic Sketches*, were annotated so
profusely as to be in themselves mines of information.

Another thing which simultaneously furnished the
poets with new material and educated the public,
was the appearance of several volumes on the Welsh
and Irish Bards. The first, and historically most important, was Evan Evans's *Specimens of the Poetry
of the Antient Welsh Bards*, which gave a tremendous
impetus to versification in English of genuine Celtic
poems of the Middle Ages. Later in the century
Edward Jones's *Musical and Poetical Relicks of the
Welsh Bards* and Joseph Walker's *Historical Memoirs
of the Irish Bards* offered more material and continued to popularize Celtic literature among the people
of England. While the poetry said to have been collected in the Highlands of Scotland by Macpherson,
Smith, Clark, and others was too freely adulterated
with spurious additions to be genuine, the discussion aroused served to advertise Gaelic poetry in a
manner most unexpected. In fact the whole Ossi-

anic controversy, of which it will be necessary to speak at some length in these pages, turned out to be one of the most successful pieces of unintentional advertising that the literary world has ever seen.

It is the aim of the following chapters to show in considerable detail the work of the five pioneers, Morris, Evans, Gray, Mason, and Macpherson, and then to enumerate, with critical comment wherever practical, the pertinent publications of the whole forty years. If the list seems to involve from time to time poems of no literary value in themselves, the generous reader will perhaps bear in mind that only by making the study as complete as possible can one give an idea of the breadth, the mass, which the movement assumed.

CHAPTER II

Lewis Morris and Evan Evans

OF all the eighteenth-century men of letters with whom we are to deal in the following pages, one of the most interesting is Lewis Morris, Llewelyn Ddu (1702–1765). He is worthy of study not only because he influenced to a considerable degree the trend of English literature, but also because he was a genius — a sort of obscure Goethe. In addition to showing as surveyor, mining engineer, and natural historian a talent that made him a marked man among his contemporaries, he was especially famous as a Welsh antiquary and poet.[1] Of his avocations he once gave a brief account in a letter to Samuel Pegge:

> . . . I should have told you also now, I am in no public business, except superintendent of the king's mines, without a salary; and that falling out with some of our leading men, I have retired into a little villa of my own, where my garden, orchard, and farm, some small mine-works, take a good part of my time, and a knowledge of

[1] For many years the facts of Lewis Morris's life were so well known to the Welsh, and so much neglected by the English, that accurate accounts were difficult to find. Recently, however, Mr. John H. Davies has published a definitive edition of *The Letters of Lewis, Richard, William and John Morris of Anglesey* (Oxford, 1906–09), with a brief but illuminating biographical Introduction.

physic and surgery, which brings me the visits of the poor; botany having been my favourite study, is now of use to *them*. Natural philosophy and mathematics have taken up much of my attention from childhood; and I have a tolerable collection of fossils, shells, etc., from most parts of the world, and a valuable collection of instruments and apparatus on that head. Models and engines also have taken up a part of my thoughts. In this branch of mechanics I have made some improvements, beyond what has been published in Britain or France. My knowledge of coins is but slender, and not worth talking of; this part of the world affording but few. I have some inscriptions found upon stones, that are curious; as also some British weapons. My collection of books is not large,[1] and they are chiefly natural history, mathematics, and antiquities of Britain.

But what has taken up my chief attention, for a good while past is, making additions to Dr. Davies' British Latin Dictionary; and also another Dictionary, entirely my own, on the plan of Mareni, which has taken up my spare hours for many years. I call it *Celtic Remains.* . . .

Welsh poetry, about twenty years ago, swam upon the surface above the rest of my store, though now sunk very low; and ever since I made some figure that way, my countrymen have thought proper, from time to time, to desire my approbation of their performances, before they showed them to the world.[2]

---

[1] The statement is more modest than accurate. For a list of the books he owned in 1760, see Additional MS. 14,955 in the British Museum.

[2] February 11, 1761. From the *Cambrian Register*, 1795, I, pp. 368–369.

One of Morris's earliest contributions toward the revival of Welsh literature was his setting up of the first printing press in North Wales for the publication of Welsh books. While there is no evidence that this venture was financially remunerative, or that he expected it to be so, he had the satisfaction of making a start.

His own Welsh poems were regarded by his countrymen as excellent, and from this judgment it is not wise for the English or American critic to dissent, especially as they have been reprinted more than a century after his death.[1] After he had proved his superiority over all the other bards of Carnarvonshire and Anglesey in a contest held in 1728, he came to be considered the leading authority on the infinitely complex subject of Welsh metrics.[2] Nor are we surprised to hear of his entertaining Lord and Lady Powys "with the actions of the Princes of Powys, and the ancient British poetry, etc., which highly delights her and diverts him."[3] Even when the pressure of his official duties left him little time for original composition, he was still consulted in a critical capacity by such a prominent poet as Evan Evans (Ieuan Brydydd Hir). When the Cymmrodorion Society of London came to select three of its

[1] The volume *Gwaith Beirdd Mon* (Liverpool, 1879) is devoted almost exclusively to the work of Lewis Morris.

[2] See Davies, *op. cit.*, p. xiii.

[3] *Ibid.*, I, p. 359.

most talented members as *bards*, Lewis Morris was among those honored.[1]

Morris's antiquarian researches, in so far as they were systematically set down, were not printed until 1878, when D. S. Evans published, from a copy of Morris's MS., part one of *Celtic Remains; or the Ancient Celtic Empire described in the English Tongue. Being a Biographical, Critical, Historical, Etymological, Chronological, and Geographical Collection of Celtic Materials towards a British History of Ancient Times. . . . By Lewis Morris, a Cambro-Briton. The Labor of 40 Years.*[2] Noteworthy as this learned volume is, it did not exert so great an influence on the eighteenth century as did Morris's English introductory essay to *Diddanwch Teuluaidd*, published in 1763.[3] A little more of his learning found its way into print during his lifetime,[4] but for the main study of his work and that of his brothers we must consult the great collection of his MSS.

---

[1] See *Cofrestr o Gymdeithas y Cymmrodorion yn Llundain* (London, 1762), p. 6.

[2] Printed for the Cambrian Archæological Association.

[3] Of special interest to the student of ballad origins are Morris's remarks about communal singing, pp. v ff. Cf. William Warrington's *History of Wales* (3d ed., 1788), pp. 316–317 for other facts about communal singing and communal composition; also Edward Jones's *Musical and Poetical Relicks of the Welsh Bards* (1st ed., 1784), p. 30.

[4] That Lewis Morris wrote the "Historical Account of the Rise of British Music" in John Parry's *Ancient British Music* (London, 1742) has not, I believe, been pointed out until now. That such is the case appears from a MS. note in Additional MS. 14,939 in the British Museum.

now in the British Museum. After turning the pages of this remarkable collection, one can but wonder that any man should in a single lifetime collect, copy, index, and annotate on so extensive a scale,[1] and with such critical acumen.

It was largely through Morris's voluminous correspondence that his influence was disseminated among Welsh and English scholars. With Thomas Carte [2] the historian, Morris carried on an extended correspondence while the former was gathering his material. Both directly and indirectly Morris seems to have been of considerable service, though in this case he received but slender acknowledgment. The extant letters being too long to quote,[3] we may substitute two extracts from letters in which Morris described the correspondence:

[To Mr. David Lewis]

What makes me dip a little now and then into the British Antiquities is, that I am egged on by a gentleman who hath very great encouragement for writing the history of Great Britain, and seeing most English writers have abused our nation, it is a pity to lose this

---

[1] Additional MSS. 14,866–14,961 in the British Museum offer almost unlimited source material for a literary biography of Lewis Morris. One collection of Welsh poetry, copied and annotated by his hand, follows another until there are nearly a hundred.

[2] It was from Carte's *History* that Gray got the tradition of the massacre of the Welsh bards, about which he wrote his great Pindaric ode, *The Bard*. See below, p. 42.

[3] See the *Cambrian Register*, II (1796), pp. 479 ff.

opportunity of vindicating ourselves, especially as I happen to have a tolerable knowledge in our histories and antiquities ... Mr. Carte, my correspondent, hath given me up many material points, particularly the Saxon letters, for which I had abundance of testimonies, besides what Mr. Edward Llwyd had. Mr. Davies of Llanerch, hath also brought him an ancient MS. in the British tongue, called Tyssilio's History of Great Britain, which Mr. Llwyd, and others, thought had been lost: — It is in the handwriting of Guttyn Owen, the poet and herald, and I have cleared the matter so to Mr. Carte, that he is the greatest advocate for the British History, as we had ... I intend (please God to give leave) to publish, sometime or other, the Natural History and Antiquities of Anglesey: Mr. Rowlands, in his Mona Antiqua, having only just raised people's curiosities.[1] I have a vast many [?] materials towards it, but want time as yet.[2]

[Lewis Morris to Samuel Pegge, February 11, 1761]

I had a correspondence formerly with Mr. Thomas Carte, for some years before he published his History of England. ... He inserted in his history several passages out of my letters, without my knowledge or consent; one of which *only* (vol. i, p. 33), he owns he had received from me. This was not good usage; for when we write letters to our friends, we are not so careful

---

[1] When the second edition of Rowlands's *Mona Antiqua restaurata* was published in 1766, it had been revised and improved immensely; "for the most of these improvements the public is indebted to the late ingenious Mr. Lewis Morris." (From the Advertisement, p. v.)

[2] From the *Cambrian Register*, 1796, II, pp. 488-489.

of the diction, as when we write to the public; and second thought may sometimes correct a former opinion.[1]

After this treatment by Carte, it is a pleasure to see that Morris fared better at the hands of Thomas Warton, who in his great *History of English Poetry* admitted his indebtedness to "an ingenious anti-quarian in British literature, Mr. Morris of Pen-bryn." [2] He corresponded also with Samuel Pegge, who "writes some curious things as an English antiquary under the name of P. Gemseage in the *Gents' Magazine*," and with Dr. Philipps, who "not being able to answer some doubts and objections of Pegge about our British History, the labouring oar falls upon me to defend our ancient History and antiquities." [3] The extant letters show that Morris was an inexhaustible source of information to other students of Welsh literature including Parry, Vaughan, and Richards.

In addition to carrying on so voluminous a cor-respondence, Morris took an active part in the work of the Cymmrodorion Society of London which met on the first Wednesday of every month at the Half-Moon Tavern on Fleet Street. An account of its transactions, tells us that it was

---

[1] *Cambrian Register*, 1795, I, p. 371.

[2] See Warton's *History of English Poetry* (1774), I, p. a4verso, note S.

[3] *Letters*, ed. Davies, II, p. 192. For further facts about the letters see *ibid.*, pp. 189–190, 201, 223, 256, 281, 344, 410; *Cambrian Regis-ter*, 1795, I, pp. 357 and 364.

originally established in London in the month of September, 1751, under the patronage of his late Majesty, at that time Prince of Wales. The object of this parent Society appears, however, according to its "Constitutions," published in 1788, to have been of a more extensive nature than those of the present [1822] Cymmrodorion; for, independent of its more immediate purpose of cultivating the language and literature of Wales, the "Constitutions" alluded to declares it to have been an additional aim of the Society to "contribute its endeavours towards the instruction of the ignorant and the relief of the distressed part of their countrymen." . . . Our present concern with the old Cymmrodorion is confined to its literary proceedings; and these appear to have been, in a great measure, directed to the collection of some scarce books and MSS. relating to Wales, and which are now in the library of the Welsh School.[1] . . . The collection of the books and MSS. already noticed must, therefore, be taken as the principal evidence of the exertions of the former Cymmrodorion, who, after an existence of about thirty years, appear to have gradually sunk into a state of inaction, that, at length, terminated in the dissolution of the Society.[2]

[1] Since Additional MSS. 14,866–14,961, already discussed (above, p. 21), were presented to the British Museum by the Governors of the Welsh School, it is probably safe to assume that the MS. collection of the old Cymmrodorion Society, later owned by the Welsh School, are the ones now in the British Museum, showing Lewis Morris's hand every few pages.

[2] This account was published in 1822 when the Society was revived, or a similar society founded as its successor. See *Transactions of the Cymmrodorion*, I (London, 1822), Preface (by J. H. Parry), pp. vi and vii.

But perhaps Morris's strongest influence was exerted through his friendship with the poets Goronwy Owen and Evan Evans. Owen he discovered, much as a manager discovers a great opera singer to-day.

When I see in Milton, Dryden, or Pope such nervous lines, and grand expressions, as this poem contains, I shall admire them as much as I do Gronow Owen, and not till then.[1]

After years of encouraging, training, and advising, he had the satisfaction of seeing many of Owen's poems published, along with his own, in the volume *Diddanwch Teuluaidd* (London, 1763), and of knowing that his protégé was making his mark among the leading Welsh poets of the eighteenth century.

His success in bringing out Evan Evans was, however, of more importance to English literature than his success with Owen; for Evans saw the necessity of putting the Welsh bards within reach of the English public. Until Morris's death in 1765 the two were close friends and corresponded frequently. When Morris died, Evans wrote to Richard that he expected to do very little with poetry in the future because, "I have *no encouragers of those studies after your brother*, and, indeed, but very few competent judges of them." [2]

[1] Lewis Morris to William Vaughan, October 7, 1752, in the *Cambrian Register*, II, 1796, p. 500.

[2] Evan Evans to Richard Morris, June 28, 1765 (*Gwaith Ieuan Brydydd Hir*, 1876, p. 196).

The work which makes Evans important in the history of the Celtic Revival was published in 1764 under the title *Some Specimens of the Poetry of the Antient Welsh Bards. Translated into English, with Explanatory Notes on the Historical Passages, and a short Account of Men and Places mentioned by the Bards.* The first part of the treatise to be completed was the *Dissertatio de Bardis*, of which he wrote to Richard Morris on October 12, 1759:

Your brother told me, when I was last at the Head, that you were going to publish G[o]ronwy's poems. If that be the case, I should be willing to contribute all in my power to render the edition complete; and for that end have wrote a Dissertation on the Bards in Latin. It consists of twenty-four leaves, wrote in the same sort of hand as you see this. I have occasionally translated some pieces of the *Gododin*, *Meilir's*, and *Cynddelw's* poems, in the same manner as those you have got already. If you have nothing of this kind by you, you may command this. It is dedicated to Mr. Vaughan of Nannau, and the other members of the Cymmrodorion Society.[1]

Six months later the *Dissertation* was being passed around among English men of letters, who apparently thought it worthy of something better than a place as an introduction to Owen's poems. Accordingly Evans wrote to Richard Morris on April 28, 1760:

[1] Evans to Morris, *ubi supra* pp. 162–163.

I have waited on Mr. Justice Barrington at Carnarvon with the *Dissertation on the Bards*, who approved of it. He has taken it and a copy of Nennius, both bound together, to London; so that I have it not in my power to send you a copy of it before next assizes, when I shall have both returned to me. He advises me by all means to translate more of the ancient Bards after the same manner I have done those odes I sent you, and make a small book of it by itself, which he says will sell well. He says that Mr. Gray of Cambridge, admires Gwalchmai's Ode to Owen Gwynedd, and I think deservedly. He says he will show the Dissertation to Mr. Gray, to have his judgment of it, and to correct it where necessary: so that I hope it will be fit for the press when I have it. I approve of your choice in your intended book, and shall be very proud of doing everything in my power to further it. But I think, with regard to the Dissertation, I had best follow Mr. Barrington's advice. . . .[1]

Thus encouraged, not only by Daines Barrington and Gray, but by Bishop Percy[2] and Richard

---

[1] Evans to Morris, *ubi supra*, pp. 164–165.

[2] To Bishop Thomas Percy is due much of the credit for the appearance of Evan Evans's *Specimens*. Percy began to write to Evans in July, 1761, and from then until at least 1776 the two men corresponded regularly on the subject of literature. Over thirty of the letters are still preserved in the British Museum (Additional MS. 32,330), yet they seem to have been wholly overlooked by historians of the Romantic movement. When Evans's volume of *Specimens* was reprinted at Llanidloes in 1862, a few of the letters, by Percy, were included as an appendix. Though very carelessly transcribed, they throw a great deal of light on the beginnings of Romanticism. The

Morris (the last of whom corrected the proof of the
Welsh poems in the *Specimens*), Evans succeeded in
getting his volume through the press in the summer of 1764.[1] The principal contents of the *Specimens* may be summarized thus:

Pages 7–57. Translation into English prose of ten
Welsh poems of which Evans has taken the originals
"from a manuscript of the learned Dr. Davies, author
of the Dictionary, which he had transcribed from an
antient vellum MS. which was wrote, partly in Edward
the second and third's time, and partly in Henry the
fifth's."[2] The titles of the poems are:

   I. Hirlas, by Owain Cyveiliog.
  II. To Myfanwy Fechan, by Howel ap Einion
     Lygliw.
 III. To Llewelyn the Great, by David Benvras.
 IV. To Llewelyn the Great, by Einion, son of Gwgan.
  V. Upon Owen Gwynedd, by Gwalchmai.
 VI. To Nest, by Einion, son of Gwalchmai.

remainder of the correspondence, equally valuable, has never been
published. While Evans was writing his book, Percy advised, encouraged, and criticized; he acted as a go-between for Evans and
Gray, and even went so far as to offer to find a publisher for the
Specimens.

[1] Prior to its publication as a part of the *Specimens*, Evans again
considered printing the *Dissertation* separately; on March 21, 1761,
he wrote Richard Morris suggesting that the latter should induce the
Cymmrodorion Society to publish it after paying Evans "ten or
eight pounds at least" for his pains in compiling it. The same letter
shows Evans's intention of showing the *Dissertation* to Lewis Morris
at Penbryn.

[2] Preface, p. iii.

VII. To Llywelyn [1] the Great, by Llywarch Brydydd
y Moch.

VIII. To Llewelyn the Great, by Llygad Gwr.

IX. The Ode of the Months, by Gwilym Ddu of
Arfon.

X. To Elphin, by Taliesin.

Pages 59–93. *De Bardis Dissertatio*, a Latin treatise
comprising the most important work of the book. The
lives and works of the principal Welsh bards are discussed at length, with numerous quotations from their
works, with Evans's translation of each into Latin. The
essay is written modestly, with no unscholarly certainty as to the exact meaning of obsolete Welsh words.
Everywhere Evans tries to show the difference between his own honest methods and the dubious methods of Macpherson.

Pages 95–151. Original Welsh versions of the ten
poems translated in the first section of the book.

The combined direct and indirect influence exerted by the *Specimens* on English men of letters
throughout the rest of the century cannot be over-
estimated. Gray put four pieces into English verse,
Richard Williams three, John Walters the Younger
three, and various other poets one each. The success of these first fruits led to translation of other
Welsh poems not given by Evans, and to imitations
almost without number. Furthermore, discriminat-
ing readers came to realize that whatever doubts
they might have about the poems of Ossian, the

---

[1] I have followed the spelling given by Evans in the titles.

works of the mediæval Welsh bards were above
suspicion.

It is to be observed that, while Evans thus furnished the matter for four of Gray's poems, —
Owen, *Hoel*, *Caradoc*, and *Conan*,[1] — he himself
wrote one English poem inspired by Gray's *Bard*.
It seems that in spite of occasional weak lines like
the third, there are many of considerable power.

A Paraphrase of the 137th Psalm. Alluding to the
Captivity and Treatment of the Welsh Bards by
King Edward I

Sad near the willowy Thames we stood,
And curs'd the inhospitable flood;
Tears such as patients weep, 'gan flow,
The silent eloquence of woe,
When Cambria rushed into our mind,   5
And pity with just vengeance joined;
Vengeance to injured Cambria due,
And pity, O ye Bards, to you.

Silent, neglected, and unstrung,
Our harps upon the willows hung,   10
That, softly sweet in Cambrian measures,
Used to sooth our souls to pleasures,
When, lo, the insulting foe appears,
And bid[s] us dry our useless tears.

"Resume your harps," the Saxons cry,   15
"And change your grief to songs of joy;
Such strains as old Taliesin sang,
What time your native mountains rang
With his wild notes, and all around
Seas, rivers, woods return'd the sound."

[1] See below, pp. 48 ff.

What! — shall the Saxons hear us sing,
Or their dull vales with Cambrian music ring?
No — let old Conway cease to flow,
Back to her source Sabrina go:
Let huge Plinlimmon hide his head,　　　　　25
Or let the tyrant strike me dead,
If I attempt to raise a song
Unmindful of my country's wrong.
What! — shall a haughty king command
Cambrians' free strain on Saxon land?　　　　30
May this right arm first wither'd be,
Ere I may touch one string to thee,
Proud monarch; nay, may instant death
Arrest my tongue and stop my breath,
If I attempt to weave a song,　　　　　35
Regardless of my country's wrong!

　　Thou God of vengeance, dost thou sleep,
When thy insulted Druids weep,
The Victor's jest,[1] the Saxon's scorn,
Unheard, unpitied, and forlorn?　　　　40
Bare thy right arm, thou God of ire,
And set their vaunted towers on fire.
Remember our inhuman foes,
When the first Edward furious rose,
And, like a whirlwind's rapid sway,　　　45
Swept armies, cities, Bards away.

　　"High on a rock o'er Conway's flood"
The last surviving poet stood,
A.d curs'd the tyrant, as he pass'd
With cruel pomp and murderous haste.　　50
What now avail our tuneful strains,
Midst savage taunts and galling chains?
Say, will the lark imprison'd sing

---

[1] I have inserted this comma, in the hope of making sense out of the passage.

So sweet, as when, on towering wing,
He wakes the songsters of the sky,   55
And tunes his notes to liberty?
Ah no, the Cambrian lyre no more
Shall sweetly sound on Arvon's shore,
No more the silver harp be won,
Ye Muses, by your favourite son;   60
Or I, even I, by glory fir'd,
Had to the honour'd prize aspir'd.
No more shall Mona's oaks be spar'd
Or Druid circle be rever'd.
On Conway's banks, and Menai's streams   65
The solitary bittern screams;
And, where was erst Llewelyn's court,
Ill-omened birds and wolves resort.
There oft at midnight's silent hour,
Near yon ivy-mantled tower,   70
By the glow-worm's twinkling fire,
Tuning his romantic lyre,
Gray's pale spectre seems to sing,
"Ruin seize thee, ruthless King."

The borrowings from *The Bard*, especially in lines
25, 47, 66, and 74, will be seen at a glance, all the
more readily because Evans himself has put the important ones in quotation marks.

Evans's various biographers cannot agree whether
his fondness for strong drink was the cause, or the
effect, of his failure to obtain promotion in the
church. However the case may have been, he fell
into bad habits and never fulfilled the expectations
of his friends as poet or critic. His success in collecting valuable Welsh MSS. did, nevertheless, stand
him in good stead, for during many years prior to

his death in 1789 he was allowed an annuity of £20 on condition that he leave all his MSS. to Paul Panton.

Anti-climactic though his literary career was, Evans lived to see the Celtic Revival in English literature in full swing. His antiquarian researches were not so deep as those of his master, Lewis Morris, and his Welsh poetry was not apparently so popular. Yet where Morris had only sown the seed among a few erudite Englishmen, Evans was able to cultivate and, by means of his *Specimens*, disseminate the flowers of Welsh literature among a much larger group. In the later chapters of this study we shall see how the work was subsequently carried on by Edward Jones, Edward Williams, William Owen Pughe, Sharon Turner, and numerous minor poets.

CHAPTER III

Thomas Gray

I

SOURCES OF GRAY'S INFORMATION

BEFORE considering further the literary relations of Evans and Gray or the influence which Gray exerted on other poets of the Celtic Revival, it may prove profitable to consider briefly the sources from which he derived his knowledge of the life and customs of the early Celts. Although he could not, apparently, read Welsh (any more than he could Norse),[1] he came to acquire a deep knowledge of Celtic origins, which, supplemented by his rare critical insight, admirably adapted him to be a leader in the new movement. While our reconstruction of the plan and extent of his research must necessarily be incomplete, it is possible to show why he was looked up to as an authority by such contemporaries as Evans and Mason.

[1] For the controversy over Gray's ability to read Norse, see E. W. Gosse, *Life of Gray*, pp. 160 ff.; G. L. Kittredge, *Gray's Knowledge of Old Norse*; C. H. Nordby, *The Influence of Old Norse Literature*, p. 5; F. E. Farley, *Scandinavian Influences in the English Romantic Movement*, p. 35, note 2; D. C. Tovey, *Gray's English Poems* (Pitt Press, 1898), p. 239, corrected in the 1911 edition.

M.ʳ GRAY.

In the first place there are several works dealing with early Celtic history, Druidism, and Welsh poetry, of which we definitely know Gray made use. Among the more important of these are the following:

Cæsar. To the account of Druidical customs given by Cæsar [*De Bello Gallico*, vi, 13–18] Gray specifically refers in his correspondence with Mason.

Tacitus. Likewise referred to familiarly in the letters to Mason. Of numerous passages about the Druids, Gray probably had in mind the *Annals*, xiv, 29–30.

R. Higden: [*Polychronicon*], cited in one of Gray's own notes to *The Bard*, 1768 edition.

Sir John Price: *Defensio Historiae Britannicae* (London, 1573), mentioned in Gray's essay "Gothi" (*Works*, ed. T. J. Mathias, 1814, II, 105).[1]

William Camden: [*Britannia*]. A tremendously popular work, first published in 1586, containing much information about the Druids. Gray, who cites the work in his notes to *The Bard* probably knew the English translation published by Edmund Gibson; of this four editions appeared between 1695 and 1772.

John David Rhys: *Cambrobrytannicae Cymraecaeve Linguae Institutiones* (London, 1592). Gray's chief

---

[1] This essay is not included by Mr. Gosse in the standard four-volume edition of Gray; hence the necessity of citing Mathias's edition. It is a most unfortunate omission, for the few pages give much evidence of Gray's reading and, incidentally, confirm Professor Kittredge's conjecture that Gray *did* know Verelius's edition of the *Hervarar Saga* (see *Gray's Knowledge of Old Norse*, p. xlv).

interest in Rhys's grammar concerned the discussion of Welsh prosody. To this treatise we find two references in his MS. essays (*Works*, ed. Mathias, II, 25 and 51); in the second case he was quoting from Carte's *History of England*, but while Carte failed to cite the page of Rhys's work, Gray looked the reference up for himself and noted "p. 146."

William Stukeley: *Stonehenge, a Temple Restored to the British Druids* (1740); and *Abury, a Temple of the British Druids, with Some Others, Described. Volume the Second* (1743). The two volumes together constitute the popular but unscholarly work on Druidism of which Gray wrote so scathingly [1] (*Letters*, ed. Tovey, II, 28–29).

Thomas Carte: *History of England*. Vol. I (1747) contains a discussion of Druidism, as well as an article by Lewis Morris on Welsh poetry from which Gray made long extracts for his own essay "Cambri" (*Works*, ed. Mathias, II, 50 ff.). Vol. II (1750) gave Gray the story of the massacre of the

---

[1] Gray wrote that a certain pamphlet was "nonsense, and that nonsense all stolen from Dr. Stukeley's book about Abury and Stonehenge." In recognizing the unscholarly nature of Stukeley's antiquarian researches, Gray was far ahead of his time. For many years the Doctor was looked up to as the greatest English authority on Druidism, but in reality his books have no value whatever. He was completely taken in by Macpherson's *Ossian*, which he said confirmed all his most important archæological discoveries (see *A Letter from Dr. Stukeley to Mr. Macpherson, On his Publication of Fingal and Temora*, London, 1763); also by the *De Situ Britanniae* attributed to Richard of Cirencester, now known to be a forgery by Bertram.

Welsh Bards by Edward I, the source of his ode
The Bard.[1]

Abbé Fénel and Nicholas Fréret: Two articles on
Druidism by these authors appeared in Vol.
XXIV of the *Mémoires de l'Acad. des belles lettres et
des inscriptions*. Gray read them both and gave
Mason a synopsis (*Letters*, ed. Tovey, II, 26–27).

Simon Pelloutier: *Histoire des Celtes* (La Haye, 1750).
Gray had read both volumes by January, 1758,
when he sent Mason a brief criticism (*Letters*, ed.
Tovey, II, 22).

J. B. B. d'Anville: *Notice de l'ancienne Gaule tirée des
monumens romains* (Paris, 1760). This valuable
treatise Gray had in his own private library.[2]

William Lambardi: *Dictionarium Angliae Topo-
graphicum et Historicum* (London, 1730). Likewise in Gray's own library.[2]

With these works we are sure Gray was familiar,
and it would be absurd to suppose that his reading
on Celtic subjects was limited to this list or to anything like it; general *a priori* considerations, combined with his nonchalant yet accurate criticisms of
Stukeley and Pelloutier, show that he was probably
equally familiar with the standard treatments of
Druidism by Humphrey Lhuyd,[3] Rowlands, To-

---

[1] See note 1, p. 42, below.

[2] See Charles Wright's *Catalogue, briefly descriptive, of various books
and original manuscripts, of the poet Gray* (London, 1851).

[3] Gray could hardly have overlooked Humphrey Lhuyd's treatise
De Mona Druidum Insula, for it is included at the end of Price's

land,[1] Borlase, and other noted Celtists. Unfortunately his intense aversion to annotating his poems, as well as the belittling way in which he always wrote in his letters of his own researches, makes it a matter of mere conjecture.[2] We may, however, be sure that he derived further information from another source — his wide circle of learned friends.

One of the most interesting of these friends was John Parry, the blind harper who inspired Gray to

Defensio in the London edition of 1573, 4to, to which Gray specifically refers.

[1] Even Mason, with his "no reading," was familiar with John Toland's delightful letters on Druidism, which were published posthumously in *A Collection of Several Pieces of Mr. John Toland* (1726), I, 1–228. Mason cites Toland in his notes to *Caractacus*, in support of a passage which Gray (*Letters*, ed. Tovey, I, 361 and note) "always admired."

[2] When Gray published *The Progress of Poesy* and *The Bard* in 1757, he wrote to Walpole: "I do not love notes, though you see I had resolved to put two or three. They are signs of weakness and obscurity. If a thing cannot be understood without them, it had better not be understood at all." With the first poem he gave no annotations whatever; with *The Bard*, four, none of which supplies any information about his Celtic reading. And when the public failed to understand him, he wrote in glee to Mason: "I would not have put another note to save the souls of all the owls in London. It is extremely well as it is — nobody understands me, and I am perfectly satisfied." In the 1768 edition he grudgingly added a few more, with the following advertisement: "When the Author first published this and the following Ode, he was advised, even by his Friends, to subjoin some few explanatory Notes; but had too much respect for the understanding of his Readers to take that liberty." The same reticence to discuss his own Celtic studies characterizes all his letters save those in which he was helping Mason with *Caractacus*.

finish *The Bard*. Parry was a famous character in his day and a great friend of the Welsh antiquary and poet, Lewis Morris. At present he is still familiarly spoken of in Wales as "Parry Ddall," and by lovers of music he will always be remembered for his three volumes of Welsh airs.[1] If not from Rhys's grammar, then it was perhaps from Parry that Gray came to understand something of the Welsh system of *cynghanedd*, which he occasionally reproduces in *The Bard*.[2] Then, too, there is the fact that by 1762

[1] *Ancient British Music . . . Part I* (1742); *A Collection of Welsh, English, and Scotch Airs, with Variations. Part II* (n. d.); *British Harmony, being a Collection of Ancient Welsh Airs . . . Part III* (1781).

[2] *Cynghanedd*, while almost equivalent to the English word "consonance," is technically used by the Welsh poets to include both consonance and certain varieties of rime; so no satisfactory translation is possible. It would, of course, be unwise to assume that Gray ever mastered the fourteen intensely complicated types of *cynghanedd*, but there are several lines in *The Bard* that reproduce the effect fairly well, and one that furnishes an absolutely perfect example of *cynghanedd draws acennog:*

Weave the wárp (and) weave the woóf.
1   2   3   4   1   2   3   4

An examination of Gray's poems shows that he used alliteration much more freely in *The Bard* than elsewhere, and it seems clear that by the use of these peculiar consonantal harmonies he was seeking to suggest a metrical system foreign to English poetry. Many Welshmen have attempted to use *cynghanedd* in English verse, but few have succeeded in producing poems of any dignity which conform strictly to the rules. The English language is so completely lacking in anything corresponding to the Welsh systems of inflection, initial mutation, and *sandhi*, that the result is almost unattainable. Had Gray reproduced the effect more perfectly, *The Bard* would necessarily have been a less successful poem.

Gray was sufficiently interested in Welsh poetry to solicit the pleasure of corresponding with Lewis Morris himself;[1] and Morris was everywhere acknowledged to be the greatest living authority on Welsh literature. Finally, we know that Gray used to confer on matters of Celtic interest with another antiquary, whose labors in this field have been commented on in the preceding chapter — no less a person than Bishop Percy.

The facts just given, while not very astonishing, go to show that Gray was more than a superficial student of Celtic antiquity. From the time when

---

[1] *The Letters of Lewis, Richard, William and John Morris, of Anglesey*, recently edited and published by Mr. J. H. Davies, contain a surprising amount of information on the interest taken by English men of letters about the middle of the eighteenth century in Welsh literature. Although there is no mention of Lewis Morris in any of Gray's extant letters, the fact that he did at least solicit his correspondence is evident from the following reference:

WILLIAM MORRIS TO RICHARD. OCTOBER 14, 1762

"In the letter I had from him [Lewis] before, of the 16th August he gave me a list of the greatest critics now in Britain who desire to correspond with him about British affairs; it seems thay are all Briton mad! Eu [h]enwau yw [i.e., their names are] Messrs. Pegge, Lye, Percy, Hurd, Shenstone, Grey [*sic*], Mason."

This letter is to be found in Vol. II, p. 511. See also *ibid.*, p. 514, for confirmation. Mr. Davies, to whom I am indebted for pointing out this item, has also called my attention to Gray's friendship with Michael Lort, Greek professor at Cambridge from 1759 to 1771. That Professor Lort corresponded frequently with the Morrises and was deeply interested in Welsh poetry, is perfectly clear (*ibid.*, pp. 537, 544, 555, 557, 565). It may be added that Professor Lort's mother was Welsh.

he began writing *The Bard* he seems to have taken a keen interest in Celtic mythology, with special reference to its use in English poetry. The outline of his projected history of English poetry shows that he was among the first to realize how great is our indebtedness to the literature of the Celts; as a writer of Celtic-English verse he was a pioneer among the early Romanticists; and the depth of his scholarship made his criticism invaluable to the poets who followed his example.

II

GRAY AND EVAN EVANS

In the preceding chapter I have said that Gray derived much of his information about Welsh poetry from Evan Evans, but it must be understood that this particular influence was not felt until after *The Bard* had been published. As the relation of these two writers is baffling, and as most of Gray's editors have been in doubt about the source of *The Bard*, it seems well to treat the problem of chronology with some detail.[1] The essential facts are these.

[1] Since the material for this chapter was gathered, I find that several of the facts about Gray and Evans have been brought to light by Professor W. Lewis Jones (*Y Beirniad*, Vol. II, No. 1). Because his essay is in Welsh, is not very comprehensive, and seems to take no account of Evans's unpublished letters in Additional MS. 32,330, I venture to cover some of the same ground.

From Vol. II of Carte's *History of England*, Gray
got all his information about the tradition of the
massacre of the Welsh bards by Edward I.[1]   Carte
in turn, as he tells us in a note, derived the story

---

[1] *The Massacre of the Welsh Bards*.   The early editors of Gray's
poems had nothing to say about the specific source of *The Bard*.
In 1894 Professor Phelps conjectured that "Gray may have met with"
the tradition in Carte's *History of England*, II, 196 (*Selections from
the Poetry and Prose of Thomas Gray*, p. 157).   Mr. Tovey (Pitt Press
edition, p. 205) said without any assurance: "Dr. Phelps thinks
Gray may have found this tradition in the second volume of Carte's
History of England, which was published in 1750."   Of course there
need not be the slightest doubt about the matter, as is obvious from
the correspondence of Evans with Bishop Percy.   Three brief quotations make it clear:

PERCY TO EVANS.   JULY 21, 1761

"P.S. I am told you are acquainted with Mr. Gray the Poet: pray
has he any foundation for what he has asserted in his Ode on the British Bard, viz., 'That there is a tradition among the inhabitants of
Wales, that our Edward Ist destroyed all the British Bards that fell
into his hands'? The existence of the tradition has been questioned."

EVANS TO PERCY.   AUGUST 8, 1761

"I have not the happiness to be acquainted with Mr. Gray. It is
very true that Edward the first destroyed the Welsh Bards, for I find
it particularly mentioned in the history of the House of Gwydir in the
county of Carnarvon, written by Sir John Wynne Bart. in the time of
Queen Eliz. who was a descendant in a direct line from the last princes
of Wales, and a person well versed in the British history in general,
and in that of his own family in particular. I have a manuscript of
this history by me. These are his words. . . ." [Here follows the
very extract from Wynne which Carte had cited in his *History*.]

PERCY TO EVANS.   OCTOBER 15, 1761

"Soon after I received your letter, I was down at Cambridge, where
I had the good fortune to meet with Mr. Gray, the poet: and spent
an afternoon with him at his Chambers. — Our discourse turned on

from Sir John Wynn[e]'s *History of the Gwedir Family*, a work not published till 1770 but accessible to him in MS. in the Mostyn library. Of so much we may be absolutely certain. It seems safe to add that some of the imagery in *The Bard* was taken from the Norse poem which Gray later translated, using Bartholin's Latin version, as *The Fatal Sisters*.[1] Evans's *Dissertation on the Bards* (which was the first part of the *Specimens* to be written) is first heard of in a letter dated October 12, 1759 — more than two years after *The Bard* had been in print.

you and the Welsh Poetry: I shewed him your Letter, and he desired leave to transcribe the passage relating to K. Edward's massacre of the Welsh bards. — All the authority he had before, it seems, was only a hint in Carte's History. He seemed very glad of this authentic report."

These three quotations are from Folios 13, 17, and 26 respectively, of Additional MS. 32,330. The first and third have already been printed in the second edition of Evans's *Specimens* (Llanidloes, 1862). For a study of the origin and spread of the tradition, references are given in Professor Phelps's *Selections*, p. 157.

[1] There can be little doubt that by 1755 Gray was familiar with Bartholin's work and was strongly influenced by it in writing *The Bard*. One of his notes to the 1768 edition suggests as much, and the fact has been hinted at by Johnson in his *Life of Gray* (cited by Professor Beers in *A History of English Romanticism in the Eighteenth Century*, p. 196); by Sayers (*Disquisitions Metaphysical and Literary*, cited by Professor Farley in *Scandinavian Influences*, p. 202); by Edward Williams, better known as Iolo Morganwg (*Poems, Lyric and Pastoral*, 1794, II, 195). The facts are clearly stated and the evidence summed up by Mr. Tovey (Pitt Press edition, pp. 212–213). His summary seems adequate, yet it may be supplemented by noting Gray's letter of March 24, 1758, where he again discusses the question of mingling Celtic and Teutonic mythology "in a time of dearth."

A single bit of Evans's Welsh poetry reached Gray shortly before April 23, 1760, but the *Dissertation* proper was not shown to him until after that date — probably in May of the same year.[1] Gray was expected, according to Evans's own statement, to "correct" the *Dissertation*, and that he took a great interest is clear from the correspondence of Percy and Evans. *The Bard* thus entirely antedates the *Specimens*, and instead of Gray's borrowing from Evans, it was the Welshman who first asked to have his work corrected by Gray. Further, it was under the direct influence of *The Bard* that Evans wrote the rather remarkable paraphrase of Psalm 137, — one of his few English poems,—which has already been quoted above, pp. 30 ff.

We may sum up the relation of the two men thus:

1755–57. Gray wrote *The Bard*, taking his Celtic material from Carte's *History* (no influence from Evans).

1759–64. Evans worked on his *Specimens*, assisted by Gray, Percy, and others, also wrote, in imitation of *The Bard*, his *Paraphrase of the 137th Psalm* (date unknown).

[1] In his letter of April 23, 1760, Evans says (*Gwaith Ieuan Brydydd Hir*, pp. 164–165) that Gray admires Gwalchmai's *Ode to Owen Gwynedd*, and that Justice Barrington will show the *Dissertation* to Gray "to have his judgment of it and to correct it where necessary." In June Gray wrote to Wharton: "The Welch Poets are also coming to light: I have seen a Discourse in MS. about them (by one Mr. Evans, a Clergyman) with specimens of their writings" (*Letters*, ed. Tovey, II, 146).

1760 or later. From the English and Latin versions in the *Specimens* (published in 1764 but seen in MS.), Gray versified *Owen*, *Hoel*, *Caradoc*, and *Conan*. The first of these four poems was printed by Gray in 1768, the others by Mason in 1775.

III

GRAY'S CELTIC-ENGLISH POEMS

The five Celtic-English poems which Gray wrote are so short that, with the omission of the long prophecy in *The Bard*, they may be included here. *The Bard*, first printed in 1757 on Horace Walpole's press at Strawberry Hill, is Gray's imaginative reconstruction of the death song of a Welsh bard who, to escape the massacre ordered by Edward I, flung himself from the top of a great precipice into the River Conway. Lines 1–8 contain the beginning of the bard's curse on Edward; lines 9–22, the description of Edward's army, and of the solitary bard far above on a cliff; lines 23–48, the bard's lament for the other bards already massacred; lines 49–100, the chorus of the spirits of the murdered bards cursing Edward and his line; lines 101–142, the solitary bard's continuation of the prophecy.

Although the tradition that Edward I ordered a massacre of the Welsh bards has now been exploded,[1] and the orthodox view that he merely

---

[1] See Thomas Stephens, *Literature of the Kymry* (2d ed.), pp. 93 ff.

issued an edict against vagrant Welsh minstrels
must be accepted, nevertheless, even casual consideration of the methods of subduing a recently
conquered people leads one to suspect that the edict
may have been enforced with unnecessary severity,
and that the conquest of Wales by Edward I may
have resulted in something approaching a massacre
of the Welsh bards.

THE BARD

I. 1

"Ruin seize thee, ruthless King!
Confusion on thy banners wait,
Tho' fann'd by Conquest's crimson wing
They mock the air with idle state.
Helm, nor Hauberk's twisted mail,
Nor even thy virtues, Tyrant, shall avail
To save thy secret soul from nightly fears,
From Cambria's curse, from Cambria's tears!"
Such were the sounds, that o'er the crested pride
Of the first Edward scatter'd wild dismay,
As down the steep of Snowdon's shaggy side
He wound with toilsome march his long array.
Stout Glo'ster stood aghast in speechless trance:
To arms! cried Mortimer, and couch'd his quiv'ring lance.

I. 2

On a rock, whose haughty brow
Frowns o'er old Conway's foaming flood,
Robed in the sable garb of woe,
With haggard eyes the Poet stood;
(Loose his beard, and hoary hair
Stream'd, like a meteor, to the troubled air)
And with a Master's hand, and Prophet's fire,
Struck the deep sorrows of his lyre.

"Hark, how each giant oak, and desert cave,
Sighs to the torrent's awful voice beneath!
O'er thee, Oh King! their hundred arms they wave,
Revenge on thee in hoarser murmurs breath;
Vocal no more, since Cambria's fatal day,
To high-born Hoel's harp, or soft Llewellyn's lay.

I. 3

Cold is Cadwallo's tongue,
That hush'd the stormy main:
Brave Urien sleeps upon his craggy bed:
Mountains, ye mourn in vain
Modred, whose magic song
Made huge Plinlimmon bow his cloud-top'd head.
On dreary Arvon's shore they lie,
Smear'd with gore, and ghastly pale:
Far, far aloof th' affrighted ravens sail;
The famish'd Eagle screams, and passes by.
Dear lost companions of my tuneful art,
Dear, as the light that visits these sad eyes,
Dear, as the ruddy drops that warm my heart,
Ye died amidst your dying country's cries —
No more I weep. They do not sleep.
On yonder cliffs, a griesly band,
I see them sit, they linger yet,
Avengers of their native land:
With me in dreadful harmony they join,
And weave with bloody hands the tissue of thy line."

II. 1

"Weave the warp, and weave the woof,
The winding-sheet of Edward's race.
Give ample room, and verge enough
The characters of hell to trace.
Mark the year, and mark the night." . . . [etc.]

[Here I omit the rest of the prophecy. The poem ends thus:]

"Be thine Despair, and scept'red Care,
   To triumph, and to die, are mine."
He spoke, and headlong from the mountain's height
Deep in the roaring tide he plung'd to endless night.

For *The Triumphs of Owen*, first published in 1768, Gray drew his material from the English prose version on pp. 25–26 of Evans's *Specimens*.

I will extol the generous hero descended from the race of Roderic, the bulwark of his country, a prince eminent for his good qualities, the glory of Britain, Owain the brave and expert in arms, a prince that neither hoardeth nor coveteth riches. — Three fleets arrived, vessels of the main, three powerful fleets of the first rate, furiously to attack him on a sudden. One from Iwerddon, the other full of well-armed Lochlynians, making a grand appearance on the floods, the third from the transmarine Normans, which was attended with an immense, though successless toil.

The Dragon of Mona's sons were so brave in action, that there was a great tumult on their furious attack, and before the prince himself, there was a vast convulsion, havock, conflict, honourable death, bloody battle, horrible consternation, and upon Tal Moelvre a thousand banners. There was an outrageous carnage, and the rage of spears, and hasty signs of violent indignation. Blood raised the tide of the Menai, and the crimson of human gore stained the brine. There were glittering cuirasses, and the agony of gashing wounds, and the mangled warriors prostrate before the chief, distinguished by his crimson lance. Lloegria was put to confusion, the contest and confusion was great, and the glory of our prince's wide-wasting sword shall be celebrated in a hundred languages to give him his merited praise.

From this uninspiring version Gray composed his poem, which he called "a fragment" — apparently because he made no use of the last few lines.

The Triumphs of Owen

(*A Fragment*)

Owen's praise demands my song,
Owen swift, and Owen strong;
Fairest flower of Roderic's stem,
Gwyneth's shield, and Britain's gem.
He nor heaps his brooded stores,
Nor on all profusely pours;
Lord of every regal art,
Liberal hand, and open heart.

Big with hosts of mighty name,
Squadrons three against him came;
This the force of Eirin hiding,
Side by side as proudly riding,
On her shadow long and gay
Lochlin plows her watry way;
There the Norman sails afar
Catch the winds, and join the war;
Black and huge along they sweep,
Burthens of the angry deep.

Dauntless on his native sands
The Dragon-Son of Mona stands;
In glitt'ring arms and glory drest,
High he rears his ruby crest.

There the thund'ring strokes begin,
There the press, and there the din;
Talymalfra's rocky shore
Echoing to the battle's roar.
Where his glowing eye-balls turn,
Thousand Banners round him burn.
Where he points his purple spear,
Hasty, hasty Rout is there,
Marking with indignant eye
Fear to stop, and shame to fly.
There Confusion, Terror's child,
Conflict fierce, and Ruin wild,
Agony, that pants for breath,
Despair, and honourable death.

Gray versified several short passages from the *Gododin* of Aneurin, of which both Welsh and Latin versions appear in Evans's *Dissertatio de Bardis*. For *The Death of Howel*, Gray used this material, leaving out, however, a long stanza. The pertinent passages in the *Specimens* (pp. 71 and 73) are these:

Si mihi liceret sententiam de Deirorum populo ferre,
Æque ac diluvium omnes una strage prostrarem;
Amicum enim amisi incautus,
Qui in resistendo firmus erat
Non petiit magnanimus dotem a socero,
Filius Ciani ex strenuo Gwyngwn ortus.

[Here follow, page 72, nine lines of which Gray made no use.]

Viri ibant ad Cattraeth, et fuere insignes,
Vinum et mulsum ex aureis poculis erat eorum potus.
—— —— —— ——[1]

---

[1] Evans puts in these dashes, apparently being unable to translate the Welsh: Blwyddyn yn erbyn wrdyn ddefawd.

Trecenti et sexaginta tres aureis torquibus insigniti erant,
Ex iis autem qui nimio potu madidi ad bellum properabant,
Non evasere nisi tres, qui sibi gladiis viam muniebant,
Sc. bellator de *Aeron* et Conanus Daearawd,
Et egomet ipse (sc. Bardus Aneurinus) sanguine rubens,
Aliter ad hoc carmen compingendum non superstes fuissem.

THE DEATH OF HOEL

Had I but the torrent's might,
With headlong rage and wild affright
Upon Deïra's squadrons hurl'd,
To rush, and sweep them from the world.

Too, too secure in youthful pride,
By them my friend, my Hoel, died,
Great Cian's son; of Madoc old
He ask'd no heaps of hoarded gold;
Alone in nature's wealth array'd,
He ask'd and had the lovely maid.

To Cattraeth's vale in glitt'ring row
Thrice two hundred warriors go;
Every warrior's manly neck
Chains of regal honour deck,
Wreath'd in many a golden link;
From the golden cup they drink
Nectar that the bees produce,
Or the grape's extatic juice.[1]

[1] It may be noted that Gray made no effort to hold his English version to anything like the simplicity of the Welsh, or to that of Evans's Latin. He could not read Welsh, but he might have conjectured that the Welsh "Gwin a medd o aur fu eu gwirawd" would be literally rendered "Wine and mead from gold was their drink." Evans's Latin is perfectly accurate except for the insertion of the unnecessary *poculis*. The literal English translation, omitting the word *was*, makes an excellent rime for *link* and would have been in other ways satisfactory. Instead, Gray made three lines out of one, getting far from the effective brevity of the original.

Flush'd with mirth and hope they burn
But none from Cattraeth's vale return,
Save Aëron brave, and Conan strong,
(Bursting through the bloody throng)
And I, the meanest of them all,
That live to weep and sing their fall.

Gray's two other fragments from the *Gododin* he likewise derived from Evans's Latin, handled even more freely than in the longer pieces. Like *Hoel*, *Conan* and *Caradoc* were first published by Mason in 1775.

CARADOC

Have ye seen the tusky boar,
Or the bull, with sullen roar,
On surrounding foes advance?
So Caradoc bore his lance.

CONAN

Conan's name, my lay, rehearse,
Build to him the lofty verse,
Sacred tribute of the bard,
Verse, the hero's sole reward.
As the flame's devouring force;
As the whirlwind in its course;
As the thunder's fiery stroke,
Glancing on the shiver'd oak;
Did the sword of Conan mow
The crimson harvest of the foe.

IV

GRAY AND MASON

William Mason's dramatic poem *Caractacus* may
be called a wholly Celtic production; the subject
is from Celtic history: the setting is Celtic; and a
distinctly Celtic atmosphere is created by the introduction of Druidism, a mythology which had
hitherto been almost wholly neglected by English
dramatists. Everyone knows what a prolific writer
Mason was, and his careless method of composition
has always been a source of amusement to men of
letters; floundering about in the unsounded depths
of Celtic antiquities, he would surely have come to
grief had it not been for the ceaseless efforts of his
painstaking friend and critic, Gray. During the
three years in which *Caractacus* was being written
Gray wrote letter after letter offering help (which
was always accepted), making suggestions, and
pointing out as tactfully as possible the absurdities
into which Mason's ignorance so often led him.[1]

---

[1] These letters are too long and too numerous to quote at length
here, but the important ones may now easily be found by reference
to the Index of Gray's *Letters, s.v.* "Mason." There are seventeen still
extant, and in many Gray goes into the most minute detail. As an
example, I quote the opening of his well-known letter of January 13,
1758:
"Dear Mason,
Why you make no more of writing an Ode, and throwing it into
the fire, than of buckling and unbuckling your shoe. I have never

So far as we can judge by his letters, Gray was much more interested in *Caractacus* than he ever was in his own *Bard;* in fact, a really fair title for the poem would be "Caractacus, a Dramatic Poem, Undertaken by William Mason and Carefully Revised by Thomas Gray." An examination of the extant letters of criticism shows that whatever merit the poem possesses is largely due to the efforts of Gray.

Although *Caractacus* was seriously underrated by its first critics,[1] nevertheless, the strange, wild

read Keysler's book, nor you neither, I believe; if you had taken that pains, I am persuaded you would have seen that his Celtic and his septentrional antiquities are two things entirely distinct. There are, indeed, some learned persons who have taken pains to confound what Cæsar and Tacitus have taken pains to separate, the old Druidical or Celtic belief, and that of the old Germans, but nobody has been so learned as to mix the Celtic religion with that of the Goths. Why, Woden himself is supposed not to have been older than Julius Cæsar; but let him have lived when he pleases, it is certain that neither he nor his Valhalla were heard of till many ages after. This is the doctrine of the Scalds, not of the Bards; these are the songs of Hengist and Horsa, a modern new-fangled belief in comparison of that which you ought to possess. . . ."

For a criticism of other early Romanticists who confused Celtic and Teutonic mythology, see above, pp. 9 ff.

[1] The critic in the *Monthly Review* for June, 1759, entirely failed to realize the importance to English literature of Mason's extensive use of Celtic mythology; at the time, the second edition was already out, yet the comment is almost entirely on the lack of dramatic action. In July of the same year a brief synopsis of the poem was printed in the *Gentleman's Magazine*, but again the reviewer had no inkling of the part *Caractacus* was to play in making the average reader familiar with the essentials of Druidism. The attitude of the *Critical Review* was even more absurd.

beauty of the Druidical elements immediately caught the public eye and aroused great enthusiasm. Some idea of its early vogue may be had from the fact that two editions appeared in 1759, and others in 1762, 1764, 1776,[1] and 1777; it was also included in vol. xxxi of Bell's *British Theatre* and in the eleven editions of Mason's poems which were published between 1764 and 1811. It was adapted for stage presentation in 1776 and was played fourteen times at Covent Garden; it reappeared two years later at the same theater, and was performed at the Felsted School, Essex, in 1785.[2] Still further evidence of the poem's popularity is afforded by the fact that it was translated into Greek, Latin, French, and Italian,[3] and was frequently imitated throughout the rest of the eighteenth century.

The source of the historical part of *Caractacus* is the *Annals of Tacitus* (XII, 33–37 and XIV, 29–30).[4] For the Celtic mythology used so freely,

---

[1] The lyrical part only.

[2] The facts about the production at Covent Garden are from Genest's *English Stage;* that it was played at the Felsted School in 1785 appears from p. 475 of the *Gentleman's Magazine* for that year, where we read: "Prologue to *Caractacus*. By Mr. Tooke, a Youth of Sixteen. Acted at the Felsted-School, Essex, April 16, 1785."

[3] All these translations are to be found in the British Museum.

[4] The material is handled so freely that it is difficult to ascertain whether any use was made of the account of the final reduction of the Island of Mona in the *Agricola*, XVIII.

Mason doubtless drew most of his information from the authors cited in the notes, which he printed "in order to support and explain some passages . . . that respect the manners of the Druids." The authors mentioned are: Am. Marcellinus, Pliny, Drayton, Rowlands (quoting from Edward Lhuyd), Dion Chrysostom, Helmodus, Tacitus, Strabo, Toland, Camden, Borlase, the Hervara Saga [!], Selden, and Lucan. A consideration of these notes, and, indeed, of the whole drama, shows that Mason was at least as well informed on Druidism as many of the minor antiquaries of his day. Worthy of special observation are his use of the sword *Trifungus* (a deliberate and pointless confusion of Teutonic and Celtic), his certainty that there were female Druids, and his doubt as to the existence of human sacrifice in Mona.[1]

In making a critical estimate of *Caractacus* it is to be noted that the chief merits of this dramatic poem lie in those features which are distinctively Celtic. Throughout the whole production there is conveyed to the reader a feeling of the solemnity and dignity of the Druidical religion which is highly pleasing. Perhaps the best idea of this can be conveyed by quoting the opening speech of the

---

[1] A long passage was originally printed explaining that such sacrifices did not exist in Mona; it was cancelled in several editions, and then reinstated, with an explanatory note, in the standard edition of 1811.

Roman general, made as he first enters the sacred
grove:

> This is the secret centre of the isle:
> Here, Romans, pause, and let the eye of wonder
> Gaze on the solemn scene: behold yon oak,
> How stern he frowns, and with his broad brown arms
> Chills the pale plain beneath him: mark yon altar,
> The dark stream brawling round its rugged base,
> These cliffs, these yawning caverns, this wide circus,
> Skirted with unhewn stone: they awe my soul,
> As if the very Genius of the place
> Himself appear'd, and with terrific tread
> Stalk'd through his drear domain. And yet, my friends,
> (If shapes like his be but the fancy's coinage)
> Surely there is a hidden power, that reigns
> 'Mid the lone majesty of untam'd nature,
> Controlling sober reason; tell me else,
> Why do these haunts of barb'rous superstition
> O'ercome me thus?   I scorn them, yet they awe me.

Slightly different in its appeal to the reader is the
lyric charm of many passages sung by the Chorus of
Bards. Of these perhaps the most beautiful is the
lament over the body of Caractacus's son, Arviragus, who died in the fight for freedom:

> I
>
> Lo! where incumbent o'er the shade
> Rome's rav'ning eagle bows his beaked head;
> Yet, while a moment fate affords,
> While yet a moment freedom stays,
> That moment, which outweighs
> Eternity's unmeasured hoards,
> Shall Mona's grateful bards employ
> To hymn their godlike hero to the sky.

II

Radiant Ruler of the day,
Pause upon thy orb sublime,
Bid this awful moment stay,
Bind it on the brow of time;
While Mona's trembling echoes sigh
To strains, that thrill when heroes die.

III

Hear our harps in accents slow,
Breathe the dignity of woe,
Solemn notes that pant and pause,
While the last majestic close
In diapason deep is drown'd;
Notes that Mona's harp should sound.

IV

See our tears in sober shower,
O'er this shrine of glory pour!
Holy tears by virtue shed,
That embalm the valiant dead;
In these our sacred songs we steep:
Tears that Mona's bards should weep.

V

Radiant Ruler, hear us call
Blessings on the god-like youth,
Who dared to fight, who dared to fall,
For Britain, freedom, and for truth.
His dying groan, his parting sigh
Was music for the gods on high;
'T was Valour's hymn to Liberty.

VI

Ring out, ye mortal strings!
Answer, thou heavenly harp, instinct with spirit all,
That o'er Andraste's throne self-warbling swings.
There where ten thousand spheres, in measured chime,

Roll their majestic melodies along,
Thou guidest the thundering song,
Poised on thy jasper arch sublime.
Yet shall thy heavenly accents deign
To mingle with our mortal strain,
And heaven and earth unite in chorus high,
While freedom wafts her champion to the sky.[1]

As another example of the lyric beauty with which
the poem abounds it may suffice to quote a part of
the ode which Gray admired because it was Druidical, and not borrowed from the Greek mythology: [2]

Mona on Snowdon calls:
Hear, thou king of mountains, hear:
    Hark, she speaks from all her strings;
    Hark, her loudest echo rings;
King of mountains, bend thy ear:
    Send thy spirits, send them soon,
    Now, when midnight and the moon
Meet upon thy front of snow:
    See, their gold and ebon rod,
    Where the sober sisters nod,
And greet in whispers sage and slow.
Snowdon mark! 'tis Magic's hour;
Now the mutter'd spell hath power;
Power to rend thy ribs of rock,
And burst thy base with thunder's shock:
But to thee no ruder spell
Shall Mona use than those that dwell
In music's secret calls, and lie
Steep'd in the stream of harmony.

[1] These lines were first written by Mason when he altered *Carac-tacus* for stage presentation in 1776. In the 1811 edition they are printed as a separate ode (*Works*, I, pp. 53 ff.).

[2] For Gray's letter, see above, p. 5, n. 3.

In addition to the solemnity of the Druidism and the musical charm of the bardic choruses, there are still two other Celtic features to which attention should be called. Brief quotations would give no adequate idea of the effectiveness of the numerous descriptions of "romantic scenery," to which *Caractacus*, like *Ossian* and many other Celtic-English poems of the period, must have owed much of its popularity.[1] Finally, the love of liberty, is harped upon so constantly that it gives the dominating tone of the drama. Even in the bardic chorus already quoted, where the champion of liberty has fallen beneath the hand of the Romans, there is a thrill of triumph in the concluding couplet:

> And heaven and earth unite in chorus high,
> While freedom wafts her champion to the sky.

V

GRAY AND MACPHERSON

Limitations of space make it impossible to do more than refer in passing to a matter of the great-

[1] Ireland, Scotland, and Wales attracted the poets of the late eighteenth century almost as much by the wild beauties of their landscapes as by their rediscovered literature. Neither the desire for the simple life nor the love of what Gray called "the savage, the rude, and the tremendous" was to be satisfied in England. An easy approach to this feature of romanticism is through the numerous popular accounts of tours through Wales, practically all of which revel in descriptions of mountain scenery.

est importance — the relation of Gray to the Ossianic poems of James Macpherson. Briefly, Gray's
influence was felt in two ways: first, his poem *The
Bard* seems to have been one of the sources of inspiration that led Macpherson to begin writing
Ossian; secondly, Gray's favorable comments on
Macpherson's earliest Ossianic efforts must have
added very considerably to the enthusiasm with
which they were received by a host of Gray's literary friends. Since it is impossible to produce all
the evidence here, it may be well to quote Mr.
Smart's phrasing of the generally accepted view of
Macpherson's direct indebtedness to *The Bard:*
"His case is the stranger because Gray, had he
looked into *Ossian* with sufficient detachment,
might have found there the influence of his own
muse. It cannot be said that had *The Bard* not
been published — it appeared in 1757 — there
would have been no *Ossian;* but *Ossian* at least
would have been somewhat different." [1] The same
opinion has been expressed with equal force by Mr.
Tovey, and the case admits of convincing (though
necessarily detailed) demonstration.

In regard to the second point, it may be said that
in spite of Gray's doubts as to the genuineness of
Ossian, he never failed to express unbounded admiration of its poetic value. He corresponded for

[1] *James Macpherson,* by J. S. Smart, p. 101.

some time with Macpherson [1] and was one of the distinguished critics who saw some of the *Fragments* in MS. before their publication in June, 1760. It has always been known in a general way that Gray's approval did much to add to the early popularity of these pieces, but attention has not, I believe, been called to the fact that an anonymous metrical version of Fragment V, contributed to the *Scots Magazine* as early as July, 1760, was, as a matter of course, given the significant subtitle, "A piece in the taste of the celebrated Mr. Gray." It is only from

---

[1] This correspondence seems to be no longer extant, but it is evident from what Gray wrote to Thomas Wharton in June, 1760, that several letters were exchanged:

"If you have seen Stonhewer he has probably told you of my old Scotch (or rather Irish) poetry. I am gone mad about them. they are said to be translation (literal & in prose) from the *Erse*-tongue, done by one Macpherson, a young Clergyman in the Highlands. he means to publish a Collection he has of these specimens of antiquity, if it be antiquity: but what plagues me is, I cannot come at any certainty on that head. I was so struck, so *extasié* with their infinite beauty, that I writ into Scotland to make a thousand enquiries. The letters I have in return are ill-wrote, ill-reasoned, unsatisfactory, calculated (one would imagine) to deceive one, & yet not cunning enough to do it cleverly. in short, the whole external evidence would make one believe these fragments (for so he calls them, tho' nothing can be more entire) counterfeit: but the internal is so strong on the other side, that I am resolved to believe them genuine, spite of the Devil & the Kirk. It is impossible to convince me, that they were invented by the same Man, that writes me these letters."

Compare also the letter of August 7, 1760, where Gray says of these same *Fragments:* "I have one (from Mr. Macpherson) which he has not printed."

a study of such incidental testimony as this, that
we can come to understand how important a part
Gray played in the Celtic Revival.

VI

GRAY AND THE MINOR POETS OF THE
CELTIC REVIVAL

We may now turn to the influence exerted by
Gray's Celtic poems on some of the minor writers of
the late eighteenth century. Out of the multitude
who took part in the movement and who were
probably affected to some extent by Gray, I have
selected a few whose indebtedness is most obvious.

One of the first and least important imitations of
Gray's *Bard* was Richard Polwhele's *Cambrian
Bards: an Ode Written about the Age of Seventeen.*
Another, *The Complaint of Cambria*, by Edward
Lovibond, contains a tribute to the Welsh bards
massacred by Edward I.

An anonymous Latin version of *The Bard* published at Chester [1] in 1775 is preceded by an English
metrical "Dedication to the Genius of Antient
Britain," which contains many phrases taken direct
from Gray's poem. Similarly, Thomas Penrose's
poem *The Harp* was so strongly influenced by *The*

---

[1] Not to be confused with the Latin version by "E. B. G.," which
was published at Cambridge in the same year.

Bard that it amounts to a selective paraphrase.[1]
And the fact that several passages in Rogers's *Ode
to Superstition* were "evidently inspired by Gray's
Bard has already been pointed out in Clayden's
Early Life of Samuel Rogers.[2]

Of considerably more interest than these are
Mathias's *Runic Odes. Imitated from the Norse
Tongue. In the Manner of Mr. Gray* (1781), of
which the fourth and fifth odes, notwithstanding
the misleading title, are not Norse but Celtic. In
the same year, 1781, John Pinkerton published his
volume of *Rimes*, conspicuous in the Celtic Revival
for the beautiful poems about Ossian. The following
lines from *The Vale of Woe, after the Gaelic Manner:*

> Heard ye not the raven scream?
> Saw ye not the sable stream?
> Heard ye not the bleak wind blow
> Adown the vale of woe?

are strongly reminiscent of Gray's fragment, *Caradoc:*

> Have ye seen the tusky boar,
> Or the bull with sullen roar,
> On surrounding foes advance?
> So Caradoc bore his lance.

[1] Penrose's poems were published posthumously in 1781, the date
of his death being 1779. For a favorable review of the volume and a
biography of Penrose, see the *European Magazine*, for March, 1782,
p. 202.

[2] Cited, with more pertinent information on the relation of Gray
to Rogers, by Professor Farley (*Scandinavian Influences*, p. 188 and
note).

Yet, after all, it may be unwise to argue that because of the striking similarity in metrical swing there is a direct imitation; the question may well be left open.

In that remarkable treatise on Welsh music, poetry, and Bardism in general, — Edward Jones's *Musical and Poetical Relicks of the Welsh Bards* [1] (1784), — the influence of Gray's Celtic interests may again be seen. The frontispiece is an engraving, after Loutherbourg, of the hero of Gray's poem, standing, harp in hand, far above the army of Edward I; and under the picture are the following lines from *The Bard:*

> On a rock, whose haughty brow
> Frowns o'er old Conway's foaming flood,
> Robed in the sable garb of woe,
> With haggard eyes the Poet stood;
> (Loose his beard, and hoary hair
> Stream'd, like a meteor, to the troubled air)
> And with a Master's hand, and Prophet's fire,
> Struck the deep sorrows of his lyre.

On page 4 are Gray's three versifications from the *Gododin,* while on page 1 is a short quotation from *Caractacus.*

Throughout the first of the two poems in his *Songs of the Aboriginal Bards of Britain,* George Richards

---

[1] The second edition, greatly enlarged, appeared in 1794, the third in 1808, and the fourth in 1825. The statement in the *D N B* that the third edition appeared in 1812 is an error. A copy of the first edition (now very rare) is in the British Museum; all the other editions, as well as a unique collection of Jones's other volumes, are to be found in the National Library of Wales, at Aberystwyth.

borrowed so freely from Gray's *Bard* that he deemed it necessary to add a note calling attention to his slight changes of Gray's imagery.

But perhaps the most astonishing result of Gray's influence on the Celtic Revival was the production in 1798 of James Boaden's historical play *Cambro-Britons*. The general subject is the invasion of Wales by Edward I, which alone would be enough to make us suspect that the author's inspiration had come from Gray. But this is not all; Act III, scene 5, of *Cambro-Britons* is from beginning to end simply a dramatization of *The Bard*, with the omission of the long prophecy. And as Genest justly remarks, this is the best scene in the play.

Another drama on the same subject was written by William Sotheby, *The Cambrian Hero, or Llewelyn the Great*.[1] Here again we have numerous lines adapted from Gray's *Bard*. Mention must also be made of *The Heroine of Cambria* (1811) by William Hayley, who had already paid his respects to the Celtic poems of Gray and Mason in his metrical *Essay on Epic Poetry*.[2] This drama, too, is based on the tradition that Edward I caused the Welsh Bards to be massacred — the same tradition that had been brought into such prominence more than fifty years before by Gray's immortal *Bard*.

---

[1] The volume is not dated, but it appeared *ca.* 1800.

[2] See Hayley's *Essay on Epic Poetry: in five epistles to the Reverend Mr. Mason* (London, 1782), *passim*, especially p. 113, where *Caractacus* is specifically mentioned.

To this list of poems deriving their inspiration
wholly or in part from the work of Gray, one might
add several anonymous pieces of some importance.[1]
And still further evidence may be found by examin-
ing the quotations and references in the countless
Tours through Wales that were published late in the
century. H. P. Wyndham, for example, wrote of the
massacre of the Welsh bards by Edward I:

If some should regret the poems, the existence of
which the massacre obstructed, they may find some
comfort in the reflection that it has given birth to one
of the finest odes in the English tongue, the merit of
which, alone, would probably surpass the ponderous
volumes of all those that might have been written in
the British language.[2]

So, too, Joseph Cradock:

. . . . for though Mona is destroyed and her Altars
abolished, — though Fires have consumed her Groves,
and her Priests have perished by the Sword, yet like
the Phoenix, she rises more glorious from Decay; her
Ashes have given Birth to the Caractacus of Mason,
and the Fate of her Bards to the Inspiration of Gray.[3]
Equally appreciative are the words of S. J. Pratt:

[1] Such as the "Ode to the Lyric Muse" (*Scots Magazine*, February,
1765); "A Poetical Chronology" by "T. M., Esq." (*Gentleman's
Magazine*, September, 1773); "Elegy on Gray" by "N" in *Poems,
Chiefly by Gentlemen of Devonshire and Cornwall* (1792).
[2] *A Tour through Monmouthshire and Wales* (2d ed., 1781), p. 149.
[3] *An Account of some of the most Romantic Parts of North Wales*
(1777), p. 64.

Neither shall I say anything of Snowdon — nor ask you to accompany me to the country, where "Huge Plinlimmon rears his cloud-topp'd head." Both of which have been introduced to you in the best manner, by Mason and Gray, the latter of whom possessed a genius loftier, and more sublime, than the mountains he described.[1]

From even so brief a study as this, it becomes evident that the Celtic Revival was dominated by the personality of the greatest poet and most careful scholar of the day — Thomas Gray. His own Celtic production was meager; but the influence of the man who wrote the *Elegy* and declined the laureateship was in no way dependent on quantity. His information was derived from a large number of sources; his influence was diffused through an even greater number of channels.

[1] *Gleanings through Wales* (3d ed., 1797), I, pp. 43–44. See also: the Introduction of William Gilpin's *Observations on the River Wye, and Several Parts of South Wales* (published 1782, 5th ed. in 1800); Richard Warner, *Walk through Wales in August 1797*, pp. 33, 84 and 155–156; Warner, *Second Walk through Wales in August and September 1798*, p. 43; Robert Potter, *Inquiry into Some Passages in Dr. Johnson's Lives of the Poets* (London, 1783), p. 30, where *The Bard* is called "the grandest and sublimest effort of the Lyric Muse." John Scott of Amwell concurred in all that Potter has said in praise of *The Bard* (*Critical Essays*, 1785, pp. 243 ff.). Such testimony can be multiplied almost indefinitely.

CHAPTER IV

James Macpherson

I

LIFE OF MACPHERSON [1]

JAMES Macpherson was born October 27, 1736. It seems that he received a good education and was expected by his friends to enter the ministry.[2] His clan took an important part in the uprising of 1745, and at the early age of nine the boy's imagination must have received a strong stimulus from the ensuing military operations. He probably entered King's College, Aberdeen, in the autumn of 1752; in any case, there is record of his formal matriculation in the following February. In 1755 he moved to the University of Edinburgh, where he seems to have been a student of divinity. In 1756 he returned to Ruthven as a schoolmaster, and, incidentally wrote several poems; among the more

[1] The chief sources used for the biography at the beginning of this chapter are: *The Life and Letters of James Macpherson*, by T. B. Saunders (1894) and the article in the *D. N. B.* by the same writer; *James Macpherson*, by J. S. Smart (1905).

[2] Gray (*Letters*, ed. Tovey, II, p. 145) wrote to Thomas Wharton of "one Macpherson, a young Clergyman in the High-lands" as the author of the poems; but apparently there is no satisfactory evidence that he ever took orders.

important are *Death*, *The Hunter*, and *The High-lander*, the last showing a striking resemblance to certain passages in *Fingal*.

From 1759 until 1763 he was engaged in collecting, writing, and publishing the volumes which have come to be known as the *Works of Ossian*. But of these more anon, in the next section of this chapter.

In 1764 Macpherson accompanied Governor Johnstone to Florida, perhaps to escape the hostility of his critics — perhaps from a natural interest in politics. On his return he was granted a pension of £200, and for some time he wrote political pamphlets in support of the government against the attacks of "Junius."

His *Introduction to the History of Great Britain and Ireland* (1771) aroused great antipathy because of its absurd glorification of the Celts. His translation of the *Iliad* (1773) added little to his fame, as Dr. Johnson's caustic reference would suggest. But in 1775 he was more successful with *Original Papers containing the Secret History of Great Britain from the Restoration to the Accession of the House of Hanover, with Memoirs of James II*, and with the *History of Great Britain from the Restoration to the Accession of the House of Hanover*. Some idea of his position at the time may be inferred from the fact that for the last of these productions the publishers paid him £3,000.

At this time Macpherson was supervising the newspapers on behalf of Lord North, for which he

JAMES MACPHERSON Esqr

received an annual stipend of £600, and in spare moments he was working on pamphlets against the Americans.

By 1780 he was a prosperous landowner, with an interest in the East Indian business of his relative Sir John Macpherson. At the same time he was receiving a secret pension of £500 from the government. When he became a Whig in the winter of 1788–1789, there seems to have been no falling off in his prosperity.

During the remaining years of his life he lived at ease, making some little effort to put into shape the so-called Gaelic "originals" of his Ossianic poems. He was still working on these when he died, February 17, 1796. The "originals" were published posthumously.

II

THE GENESIS OF OSSIAN

In the January issue of the *Scots Magazine* for 1756 appeared the following letter from Jerome Stone, which probably came to Macpherson's attention, or at least caused a discussion of Celtic poetry in which he took part:

Sir, —   DUNKELD, Nov. 15, 1755.

Those who have any tolerable acquaintance with the *Irish* language, must know, that there are a great number of poetical compositions in it, and some of them

of very great antiquity, whose merit entitles them to
exemption from the unfortunate neglect, or rather
abhorrence, to which ignorance has subjected that
emphatic and venerable language in which they were
composed. Several of these performances are to be met
with, which for sublimity of sentiment, nervousness of
expression, and high-spirited metaphors, are hardly to
be equalled among the chief productions of the most
cultivated nations. Others of them breathe such ten-
derness and simplicity, as must be greatly affecting to
every mind that is in the least tinctured with softer
passions of pity and humanity. Of this kind is the poem
of which I here send you a translation. Your learned
readers will easily discover the conformity there is,
betwixt the tale upon which it is built, and the story of
Bellerophon, as related by *Homer*; while it will be no
small gratification to the curiosity of some, to see the
different manner in which a subject of the same nature
is handled, by the great father of poetry, and a highland bard. It is hoped, the uncommon turn of several
expressions, and the seeming extravagance there is in
some of the comparisons I have preserved in the translations, will give no offence to such persons as can form
a just notion of those compositions, which are the production of simple and unassisted genius, in which energy
is always more sought after than neatness, and the
strictness of connection less adverted to, than the design of moving the passions, and affecting the heart.

I am, etc.

[Here follow twenty ten-line stanzas, entitled
Albin and the Daughter of May: An old tale, trans-

lated from the Irish. Most of the poem deals with
the death of Albin, who is beguiled by the mother
of his mistress into fighting a venomous dragon.
With some of the laments in Macpherson's work it
may prove interesting to compare the last stanza]:

> But now he's gone! and nought remains but woe
>   For wretched me; with him my joys are fled,
> Around his tomb my tears shall ever flow,
>   The rock my dwelling, and the clay my bed!
> Ye maids, and matrons, from your hills descend,
>   To join my moan, and answer tear for tear;
> With me the hero to his grave attend,
>   And sing the songs of mourning round his bier.
> Through his own grove his praise we will proclaim,
> And bid the place forever bear his name.

Whatever influence Jerome Stone [1] may have had
on Macpherson, it is certain that before the end of
the year 1759 the latter had made a small collection
of popular Gaelic poems. An interest in the matter
being expressed by John Home, author of *Douglas*,
Macpherson consented to show him some of the
poems in his possession. It now seems definitely
established that Macpherson deliberately palmed
off on his friend a remarkable composition of his
own, *The Death of Oscar*, under the pretense that it
was a literal translation of an old Gaelic poem.[2]

---

[1] For important facts about the life and works of Stone, see D.
Mackinnon's article in the *Transactions of the Gaelic Society of Inverness*, XIV, pp. 314–369.

[2] See *James Macpherson*, by J. S. Smart, pp. 89–93.

Struck by the strangeness and beauty of the piece, Home obtained more "translations," with which he was soon able to enrapture the literary circle of Edinburgh. As the leading Scottish dramatist of the day, Home naturally had some influence with such men of letters as David Hume, Dr. Carlyle, and Hugh Blair; and to them he communicated his discovery. After this the poems circulated in MS. for some time, and were sent by Sir David Dalrymple to Horace Walpole at Strawberry Hill. To some extent they doubtless circulated among the English *literati*, and were certainly read by Thomas Gray.

At the instigation of his friends, especially Hugh Blair, Macpherson published anonymously, in June, 1760, a booklet of seventy pages, entitled *Fragments of Ancient Poetry, Collected in the Highlands of Scotland, and Translated from the Galic or Erse Language*. It contains a short, unsigned Preface by Hugh Blair, and fifteen "Fragments" in English prose of peculiar rhythmic charm. The success of the book was immediate; favorable reviews appeared in the *Monthly* and the *Critical*; long extracts and numerous arrangements in verse were printed in the *Gentleman's Magazine* and the *Scots Magazine*.[1] Before the year was out, a second edition, with one additional piece, had appeared.

Immediately a subscription was taken to enable Macpherson to make two trips to the Highlands and

[1] See below, p. 93.

to the Islands of the West, to collect more Gaelic poetry. From the genuine material thus gathered Macpherson composed — mixing about six parts of his own imagination with one of Gaelic ballad — the long poems *Fingal* and *Temora*. On publishing them in 1761 [1] and 1763 respectively, he took every possible precaution against the discovery of his forgery, loading the poems with introductions and notes amounting in all to several hundred pages. *Fingal* he signed as translator, and *Temora* he signed and dedicated to his influential patron, the Earl of Bute. With the latter volume he was able to include seventeen pages of Gaelic as a "Specimen of the Original of Temora." [2] Such was the genesis of Macpherson's *Ossian*, which proved to be the most influential production of the Celtic Revival, and which aroused the bitterest literary controversy of the eighteenth century.

III

THE VOGUE OF *OSSIAN*

The success of *Ossian* both in Great Britain and on the Continent was greater than Macpherson could have anticipated in his most optimistic mo-

[1] The title page of *Fingal* bears the date 1762, but that it was out by December 31, 1761, is evident from Horace Walpole's letter of that date (*Letters*, ed. Mrs. Paget Toynbee, V, 150).

[2] For observations on the genuineness of this specimen, see below, pp. 78 ff.

ments. To make a bibliography of all the editions in English from 1760 to 1800 has proved a greater task than I can hope to complete for many years, and the list I submit, lacking as it is in data about the number of copies in each edition, is by no means satisfactory. It does, however, suggest that the poems had an amazing vogue, and it may prove a stepping-stone toward something more useful.

SEPARATE EDITIONS OF THE *Fragments*

1760. Edinburgh. Two separate editions.
1761. London. (A reprint from the 2d edition, in Dodsley's *Fugitive Pieces on various subjects*, II.)
1762. Dublin.
1765. London.
1771. London. Called the "Third edition."

SEPARATE EDITIONS OF *Fingal*, etc.

1762. London. Two separate editions, the first actually appearing at the end of 1761.
1762. Dublin. (Apparently printed after the first London ed., as might be expected. See pp. 4–5 of Ferdinando Warner's *Remarks on the History of Fingal* (London, 1762).)
1788. Gottingue. (Contains *Fingal* only — not the short poems usually included with it.)

SEPARATE EDITIONS OF *Temora*, ETC.

1763. London.
1763. Dublin.

THE COLLECTED *Poems* (OR *Works*) *of Oṣsian*

1765 London. 2 vols. "Third edition." (Probably so called because *Fingal* and *Temora* had appeared before. This seems to be the first complete edition.)
1773. London. 2 vols.

1773–75. Darmstadt. 2 vols.
1777. Francfort and Leipzig. 4 vols.
1783. Francfort and Leipzig. 4 vols.
1783. Paris. 4 vols.
1784. Nürnberg. (Extracts only, in *Tales of Ossian for Use and Entertainment. Ein Lesebuch für Anfänger im Englischen.*)
1785. London.
1789. London. (Extracts only, edited by Miss Potter.)
1790. Dublin. 2 vols.
1790. Philadelphia.
1792. Edinburgh. 2 vols.
1794. Nürnberg. (2d and enlarged edition of *Tales of Ossian,* etc. Cf. 1784.)
1795. Perth. 2 vols.
1795. Berwick. 2 vols.
1796. London. 2 vols.
1797. Edinburgh. 2 vols.

Add to this list the dramatizations, imitations, and metrical versions cited in Chapters V to VIII of this study; estimate roughly the number of extracts in magazines and newspapers; add the almost countless controversial pamphlets and criticisms, and the popularity of *Ossian* in Great Britain can be vaguely appreciated.

On the Continent the popularity of *Ossian* was equally surprising. Within a short time it was translated into German, Italian, Spanish, French, Dutch, Danish, Swedish, Polish, and Russian.[1] Its influence on European literature was so universal as to baffle critical analysis; four volumes have been

---

[1] *James Macpherson,* by J. S. Smart, p. 11.

devoted to *Ossian's* triumphs in Germany, France, and Italy; but admirable as these studies are, they do not, together, cover more than half the field of European letters.[1] From my own limited observation I judge that one long quotation from *Ossian* near the end of Goethe's *Werther* (1774) did more to spread the Ossianic fever than can now be estimated. Striking examples of this sort may be multiplied almost indefinitely.

IV

THE OSSIANIC CONTROVERSY

From the first appearance of Macpherson's *Fragments of Ancient Poetry* in 1760, there was serious doubt in the minds of many as to whether the poems were, as Macpherson said, literal translations of pieces composed by Highland bards and handed down by oral tradition. With the publication of his elaborate epics *Fingal* and *Temora*, and his failure to publish or show the Gaelic "originals" (except for a few pages printed with *Temora*), the situation

[1] See Karl Weitenauer's München dissertation, *Ossian in der italienischen Litteratur bis etwa 1832, vorwiegend bei Monti* (1905); Rudolf Tombo, Jr.'s Columbia dissertation, *Ossian in Germany* (1901); A. Tedeschi's *Ossian "L'Homère du Nord" en France* (Milan, 1911); and P. Van Tieghem's *Ossian en France*. For the enthusiasm of Goethe, Klopstock, and Herder for Ossian, see the first paragraph of Kuno Meyer's article in *Abhandlungen der königl. preuss. Academie der Wissenschaften* (1913).

became increasingly embarrassing for him and his friends. The controversy waxed more bitter and complex until 1807, when, with the publication of all the Gaelic MSS. purporting to be the originals, the problem was reduced to a definite, tangible question: Did Macpherson write the Gaelic version first or, as his enemies said, the English?

To trace the history of the whole controversy would fill many volumes, but a summary may be included here to advantage. As has been intimated, Hugh Blair, famous for both his sermons and his lectures on rhetoric, was an ardent supporter. He wrote the Preface for the *Fragments*, and his *Critical Dissertation* [1] was among the most influential of the early essays. To the end of his life Blair supported Macpherson's cause vigorously. William Stukeley, the antiquary, was equally strong in his *Letter from Dr. Stukeley to Mr. Macpherson, on his publication of Fingal and Temora* (London, 1763). He explained at length how *Ossian* had confirmed many of his favorite archæological theories, and how "the world is highly obliged to you [Macpherson] for preserving so noble, so interesting a monument of high

---

[1] *A Critical Dissertation on the Poems of Ossian, the Son of Fingal* (London, 1763). Probably this was the most influential document in the whole discussion until Laing's arguments on the other side appeared early in the nineteenth century. It was included in almost every edition of *Ossian* in English, as well as many in German. The substance of the *Dissertation* was originally delivered in his lectures at the University of Edinburgh.

antiquity." [1] John Pinkerton believed for some time in the genuineness of the work, but subsequently changed his opinion. [2] John Home was a loyal supporter, to whom Macpherson owed much of his success. Home even went so far as to dramatize a part of *Ossian* in his *Fatal Discovery*. [3]

Horace Walpole, very enthusiastic at one time, soon came to doubt the reliability of Macpherson and to write of the poems with the utmost contempt. [4] But the most influential of Macpherson's opponents was Dr. Johnson, whom the angry Scot finally challenged to a duel. [5] Probably it is safe to say that Johnson, like Wordsworth, found in the very style of the "translations" sufficient evidence to persuade him they were spurious. [6]

The problem of suggesting the extent of a controversy in which almost every critic of the day

[1] Page 6.   [2] Cf. below, p. 132.   [3] See below, p. 100.

[4] Compare the letter of April 14, 1761, where he says "My doubts of the genuineness are all vanished," with that of February 7, 1777: " . . . what difficulty is there in believing that Macpherson forged the cold skeleton of an epic poem, that is more insipid than Leonidas?" Also the letter of June 25, 1782: Epic poetry "has continued to degenerate from the founder of the family, and happily expired in the last bastard of the race, Ossian." For these and numerous other references to Ossian, see Mrs. Paget Toynbee's edition of the *Letters* (Oxford, 1904), V, p. 50; X, p. 15; XII, p. 274; and the Index.

[5] One of the few places where Johnson's famous reply is quoted accurately is in Saunders's *Life and Letters of James Macpherson*, pp. 250-251.

[6] See Wordsworth's *Essay, Supplementary to the Preface of the Lyrical Ballads* (1815).

took part, may be simplified by quoting the excellent bibliography prepared by L. C. Stern. It includes only the more important items, and in this selected list I have taken the liberty of marking with an asterisk names that are of special note. In other respects Stern's list is reprinted below as it stands on pp. 261–262 of his article in the *Transactions of the Gaelic Society of Inverness* for 1897–1898.[1]

Among the champions of "Ossian" may be named:

*H. Blair, 1763; *M. Cesarotti, 1763; J. Wodrow, 1771; J. G. Sulzer, 1771; Whitaker, 1773; *Th. Warton, 1774; H. Home, Lord Kaimes, 1775; *W. Shaw, 1778; D. Macnicol, 1779; M. Dorat, 1780; *J. Smith, 1780; *J. Clark, 1782; J. L. Buchanan, 1793–94; L. W. Flügge, 1796; Alex. Campbell, 1797; C. H. Schundenius, 1799; J. Macdonald, 1802; J. Curlitt, 1802; Mrs. Grant Laggan, 1803; Arch. Macdonald, 1805; P. Graham, 1807; *Sir John Sinclair, 1807; J. Grant, 1814; E. Maclachlan, 1818; *H. and J. MacCallum, 1816; Alex. Macdonald, 1820; H. Campbell, 1822; J. Lyon, 1821; J. Reid, 1832; P. Macgregor, 1841; Clemen, 1854; Oswald, 1857; *Thos. Maclauchlan, 1857; P. Macnaughton, 1861; D. Campbell, 1862; *J. F. Campbell, 1862; *W. F. Skene, 1862; E. Waag, 1863; Th. Pattison, 1866; Arch. M'Neil, 1868; A. Ebrard, 1868–70; *Arch. Clerk, 1870; P. H. Waddell, 1875; J. St. Blackie, 1876; C. S. Jerram, 1876; D. Mackinnon, 1877; *Shairp, 1880; Ch. Stewart, 1884; *Alex. Mac-

[1] See Zt. f. vergl. Littgesch. N. F. VIII (1895) for the original.

bain, 1884. The many translators of "Ossian" who seem by this to be convinced of its genuineness I have not mentioned in the above list.

Doubt in the genuineness of the *Poems of Ossian* is met with in 1762 in the *Journal of Sçavants*, Nov., pp. 724 ff.; then follow in the same line the critic of 1764 and *F. Warner, *Ch. O'Conor, 1766–75; *S. Johnson, 1775; Sir James Foulis, *W. Shaw, 1781–84; *M. Laing, 1800–05; *Th. O'Flanagan, 1808; Fink, 1811; Ch. O'Conor, d. J., 1814; Edw. Davies, 1825; W. H. Drummond, 1831; *Edw. O'Reilly, 1831; *Talvj (Therese Ad. L. v. Jacob), 1840; *O. Connellan, 1860; *E. O'Curry, 1862; the "Times," 1869; *W. M. Hennesy, 1871; *J. F. Campbell, 1872; *St. H. O'Grady, 1880; *Alex. Macbain, 1886–87; H. Maclean, 1887; *Professor Mackinnon, 1890; *Alf. Nutt, 1890; H. D'Arbois de Jubainville, 1892. Here, as in the foregoing note, only the most important names are given, for a complete Ossianic bibliography would of itself fill a volume.

The end of the Ossianic controversy did not come until near the close of the nineteenth century. It will be seen from an examination of Stern's lists just quoted, that many a noted scholar changed his opinion from one of belief to one of doubt. In 1872 J. F. Campbell, one of the most learned of these, published his great *Leabhar na Feinne*, a collection of Gaelic ballads so important that its editor was at once marked as better qualified than almost any other critic to speak on the authenticity of Mac-

pherson's work. His opinion is stated succinctly
page 33:

I now believe that MacPherson's *Ossian* is a great
original work of fiction, dating from 1760, when it appeared in print; and that the Gaelic of 1807 is one of
many translations.

In the *Celtic Magazine* for 1886–1887 there appeared a series of articles by the editor, Alexander
Macbain, who was one of the greatest authorities on
the linguistic questions at issue. His unfavorable
opinion is expressed with the utmost vigor, and in
no particular is there any possible doubt as to the
accuracy of the evidence he arrays against Macpherson. His article may be briefly summarized as
follows:

Pages 145–150. The historical background of the
poems shows conclusively that they were the invention
of someone ignorant of early Celtic history. Many of
the proper names are obvious fabrications; the name
Fingal itself cannot be accounted for satisfactorily.

Pages 151–154. The life portrayed in *Ossian* is absolutely at variance with all that we know of the manners and customs of the Celts. (Cf. pp. 195–199.)

Pages 193–194. There is a deadly resemblance to
The Highlander, which Macpherson published in 1758.

Pages 199–248. The most incisive criticism yet made
of the absurd mythology, humorously incorrect grammar, and the verse structure of Macpherson's Ossianic
poems, especially as shown in the Gaelic version of 1807.

Page 250. A list of "gems," over which Macbain waxes sarcastic; also a list of absurd "Anglo-Classicisms."

Page 252. "Which is the translation, the Gaelic, or the English? The Gaelic is the translation. Or rather, we should say the English was first written, and thereafter Gaelic poetry on the same subject was written, closely following the English in general plot and idea."

Page 254. "He did not, like Tennyson, merely give a new and modern rendering of old tales and ballads. Scarcely a third of his whole Ossianic work has any authentic counterpart, such as it is, in the ballads. The rest is absolutely his own work. In fact, the ballads cannot count seriously in our estimate of Macpherson as a poet. His 'Ossian' is as truly his own work as ever that of any great poet has been the work of that poet."

Finally came L. C. Stern's article *Die Ossianischen Heldenlieder,* which was published in Koch's *Zeitschrift.*[1] This was at once accepted by the chief Celtic scholars as standard, was translated into English by J. L. Robertson, and read before the Gaelic Society of Inverness by Alexander Macbain. It leaves no doubt that the Gaelic "original" of *Ossian* is nothing but a poor translation from the English.

About the best brief summary of the situation has been given by Alfred Nutt in his *Ossian and the Ossianic Literature:*

[1] N. F., VIII.

He [Macpherson] undoubtedly had some knowledge of the Ossianic ballad literature existing in the Highlands in his day, and he worked up many of its themes into his English Ossian, which is, however, almost as much his own composition as "Paradise Lost" is the composition of Milton. . . . For the student, whether of Celtic myth and saga, of Celtic archaeology, or of Gaelic style and literary form, Macpherson's poems are worthless; they disregard the traditional versions of the legends, they depart from the traditional representation of the material life depicted in the old and genuine texts, and they utterly ignore the traditional conventions of Gaelic style.[1]

The influence of *Ossian* on eighteenth-century literature was doubtless affected by the bitterness of the controversy. Men like Gray, for instance, hesitated to write imitations when they knew that by so doing they would expose themselves to the attack and even the ridicule of a large number of critics. On the other hand, the heat of the discussion tended to make the supporters of Macpherson all the more ardent, and the imitators all the more enthusiastic. On the whole, I am inclined to think that the controversy did more to encourage imitation than to prevent it.

[1] Pages 1–2. See also the excellent summary given by E. C. Quiggin in the *Encyclopædia Britannica* (11th ed.), V, pp. 637–638.

V

CRITICAL ESTIMATE OF *OSSIAN*

The question now arises, what is Macpherson's place in the whole great movement called the Celtic Revival of the eighteenth century? To what extent was the appeal of his Ossianic poems due to the fact that they were Celtic, and to what extent to other causes? Most Celtic-English poetry of the same period appealed to the public because of certain features that were essentially Celtic; does the same remark apply to *Ossian*? An answer to these questions must fall under at least four separate headings.

First, the most obvious appeal of Celtic poetry was the change it offered from classical mythology, which had been worn threadbare by constant use. Here Macpherson made only slight use of his opportunity. Although the heroes of his poems are different in type from the conventional Greek heroes, the mythology of the Druids is neglected in *Ossian*. The supernatural effects he produces are amorphous, cloudy spirits hovering around, waiting to be sung to, and generally in the reader's way. Of the majesty of Druidism, the awe-inspiring rites of the white-robed priests, of the amazing religious and political influence they wielded, there is nothing. Even Mason could do better, and did better.

A second feature of the Celtic Revival was the

part it played in satisfying the popular desire for a return to the primitive. This desire, so common among highly developed civilizations, had become, under the influence of Rousseau and others, a veritable mania, of which the most interesting symptom was perhaps the number of poems about the American Indians. In satisfying this taste for the primitive, Macpherson's work was successful for a time; the strong elemental passions of the ancient Celts are set forth to advantage. In so far, then, as the Celtic Revival was a result of the "back to nature" movement, *Ossian* leaves little to be desired.

In the third place Macpherson seems to have been fully aware of the newly awakened interest in what was called "romantic scenery." But here he has achieved an effect that is quantitative rather than qualitative. That is to say, rocks, waves, clouds, and mountains are referred to on almost every page of *Fingal*, yet the imagery is seldom definite enough to convey anything more than a vague impression. This lack was felt keenly by Wordsworth:

Having had the good fortune to be born and reared in a mountainous country, from my very childhood I have felt the falsehood that pervades the volumes imposed on the world under the name of Ossian. From what I saw with my own eyes, I knew that the imagery was spurious. In nature everything is distinct, yet nothing defined into absolute independent singleness. In Macpherson's work, it is exactly the reverse; everything (that is not stolen) is in this manner defined, insulated, dislocated, deadened — yet nothing distinct. It will always be so when words are substituted for things.[1]

And though Poe keenly resented this attack on what he called "this gorgeous, yet simple imagery, where all is alive and panting with immortality," [2] one has but to turn the pages of *Ossian* to see that in the majority of cases Wordsworth was right. In brief, the descriptions of landscapes and of the majesty of nature are numerous rather than effective.

Finally, most of the Celtic-English poetry appealed to the love of liberty. In an age when the agitation against slavery was first assuming importance and the great struggle for freedom was reaching its climax in France and America, it is not strange that people should have glorified the Celts, whose struggles to retain their freedom in spite of the inroads of more powerful nations have been uninterrupted. In fact, the Celtic-English poetry of the age (except for Macpherson's) is chiefly marked by reference to the love of liberty. Sometimes this theme is used as the subject of a poem; sometimes there is only an illustrative reference; but the poets never tired of harping on it, and the public never tired of listening. In this respect, how-

[1] From the *Essay Supplementary to the Preface of the Lyrical Ballads* (1815).

[2] In the Introduction to the 1831 edition of his own poems.

ever, Macpherson is lamentably lacking. For the love of liberty, he substituted a melancholy tone of regret — regret for anything and everything. So prominent is this characteristic that to anyone who is even slightly familiar with the genuine traditional literature of the Celts, the only phrase adequate to describe the mood of *Ossian* is *morbid sentimentalism*. If there is any one sentence that perfectly misrepresents the genuine Celtic spirit, it is this:

They went forth to the war, but they always fell.

As a representative poet of the Celts, Macpherson was not, then, a great success. He failed to avail himself of Druidism; he did set forth the primitive passions and the primitive simplicity of life in the Highlands in a way to interest his contemporaries; he loaded his poems with descriptions, of doubtful literary value; and for the traditional Celtic love of liberty he substituted a morbid melancholy.

Why then were his Ossianic poems so popular? Perhaps because of this very sentimentalism. In an age when every "genteel" person was expected to be able to shed "a feeling tear" on any occasion, when readers of all classes sighed over the *Sentimental Journey*, wept over *Pamela*, contemplated suicide with Werther, and shuddered over the cheap claptrap of *The Castle of Otranto*, the public found just what it wanted in the gloomy pages of *Ossian*. Whatever we may say of Macpherson's honesty, we must admit that, as a canny Scot, he was perfectly capable of feeling the pulse of his own age. His poems contain a tragic gloom by no means unpleasant to the eighteenth-century sentimentalist, or perhaps to the modern reader who limits himself to a few pages. But the present age, still interested in genuine Celtic sagas, has tired of the unnatural preponderance of melancholy under which *Ossian* groans. To the twentieth century, Macpherson is no more. "Let the joy of his grief be great!" [1]

If any further cause for the popularity of *Ossian* is needed, it may perhaps be found in the novelty of Macpherson's "measured prose." His style is not merely highly imaginative, or merely pleasing in occasional rhythmic cadences; it contains numerous

[1] It is to be regretted that Matthew Arnold, in his essay on *The Study of Celtic Literature*, was so seriously led astray regarding the general tone of Celtic literature. The "chord of penetrating passion and melancholy" which he found in Macpherson's *Ossian* was only a sentimental discord quite out of harmony with the vivacity, and even the humor, of the genuine sagas.

Although most of Arnold's worst blunders of fact have been corrected in the Preface, Introduction, and notes of Alfred Nutt's edition of the essay (1910), and in J. S. Smart's *James Macpherson* (pp. 20–28), apparently no one has yet pointed out that Arnold plainly argues in a circle concerning melancholy. On p. 90 (Nutt's edition) he argues that melancholy, since he finds it in Macpherson's *Ossian*, is distinctly Celtic, and by p. 113 he makes it one of the three leading traits of Celtic literature. Then, fearing that the reader will question the argument based on Macpherson's poems, he assures us (p. 128) that they contain "the very soul of the Celtic genius" because they so persistently emphasize this very quality of melancholy. Such logic needs no refutation.

sentences, and even paragraphs, that divide themselves inevitably into the recognized feet of English
poetry. While we cannot say that all of *Ossian* was
written in unrimed verse printed like prose, we can
say that much of it was, and that the average is
nearer to poetry than to prose. Two passages
picked at random from the first books of *Fingal* and
Temora respectively, will illustrate the effect more
clearly than any exposition could do. Only a little
change in the printing is necessary to show that
these lines are rhythmically far superior to most
modern examples of *vers libre*.

> It bends like a wave near a rock;
> Like the golden mist of the heath.
> Its sides are embossed with stones,
> And sparkle like the sea round the boat of night.
> Of polished yew is its beam,
> And its seat of the smoothest stone.
> The sides are replenished with spears;
> And the bottom is the foot-stool of heroes.
>
> [*Fingal*, 1st ed., p. 11.]

> The king, at length, resumed his soul,
> And took his pointed spear.
> He turned his eyes to Moi-lena.
> The scouts of blue ocean came.
> They came with steps of fear,
> And often looked behind.
> Cairbar knew that the mighty were near,
> And called his gloomy chiefs.
>
> [*Temora*, 1st ed., p. 5.]

The effect of this "measured prose" has been discussed by many leading critics, — notably by Pro-

fessor Saintsbury, — and it is generally agreed that Macpherson owed much of his success to this violent revolt from the closed couplet of Pope and the classical school.[1] Had he broken the lines off short to emphasize the rhythm (as in the arrangement just above), he would have called attention also to the prosaic nature of many less carefully "measured" sentences. But by printing as prose, he left the reader to discover for himself the unexpected charm of the more rhythmic passages.

[1] See George Saintsbury, *A History of English Prosody*, III, pp. 43–46; *A History of English Prose Rhythm*, pp. 469–471.

FRAGMENTS

OF

ANCIENT POETRY,

Collected in the Highlands of Scotland,

AND

Tranſlated from the Galic or Erſe Language.

Vos quoque qui fortes animas, belloque peremtas
Laudibus in longum vates dimittitis ævum,
Plurima ſecuti fudiſtis carmina Bardi.

LUCAN.

EDINBURGH:

Printed for G. HAMILTON and J. BALFOUR.
MDCCLX.

CHAPTER V

1760-1770

"THERE can be perhaps no greater entertainment than to compare the rude Celtic simplicity with modern refinement," wrote Goldsmith,
expressing the interest of his contemporaries in the
Celts — an interest amounting to more than mere
curiosity, as we see from a statement in the same
essay that the songs of the Irish bard Carolan "may
be compared to those of Pindar, as they have the
same flights of imagination."

No doubt it was with some such combination of
antiquarian and artistic interest that the public
looked on Macpherson's *Fragments* and on the numerous versifications of them in 1760 and the years
following. Hardly a month after Macpherson's
little volume had appeared, both the *Scots Magazine*
and the *Gentleman's Magazine* produced rival versifications, and within a short time we find six anonymous poets putting the first of *Ossian* into verse,[1]
for example:

---

[1] See the *Scots Magazine*, July, 1760, pp. 360–362; the *Gentleman's
Magazine*, July, 1760, p. 335, and February, 1761, p. 89; the *Monthly
Review*, September, 1760, pp. 210–211; the *Annual Register*, 1760,
pp. 227–228. My quotation is from the first.

Swift wert thou, Morar, as the bounding roe,
As fiery meteors dreadful to the foe.
Like winter's rage was thine, in storms reveal'd;
Thy sword in fight like lightning in the field;
Thy voice like torrents swell'd with hasty rains,
Or thunder rolling o'er the distant plains:
Unnumber'd heroes has thy arm o'erturn'd;
In smoke they vanished when thy anger burn'd.

The approval of Macpherson's Ossianic poems implied in the publication of such versifications was not enough for the enthusiastic editors of the *Annual Register*. In their volume for 1761 they gave five pages to quotations from arrangements in various meters of the *Songs of Selma*,[1] and ten pages to a review of Macpherson's *Fingal*. It is hard to realize to-day that, before the opposition to *Ossian* had crystallized, serious people were forming their literary opinions from reviews beginning like this:

From the publication of these extraordinary poems, the ingenious editor has a double claim to literary applause. One, as having with equal industry and taste recovered from the obscurity of barbarism, the rust of fifteen hundred years, and the last breath of a dying language, these inestimable relics of the genuine spirit of poetry: and the other, for presenting them to the world in an English translation, whose expressive singularity evidently retains the majestick air, and native simplicity of a sublime original. The venerable author,

[1] Pages 270–275.

and his elegant translator, thus have mutually con-
ferred immortality on each other.[1]

In view of the fact that Macpherson's *Songs of
Selma* did not appear until December, 1760, it is
remarkable that in January of the following year
there should have been published *The Songs of
Selma. From the Original of Ossian the Son of Fingal*
(London). It was very favorably reviewed on pages
78–80 of the *Monthly* for January, but I do not know
that the author's name was ever discovered. The
work consists of a rendering into heroic couplets
and various ballad meters of the *Songs of Selma*,
which Macpherson had published in "measured
prose" along with his *Fingal*. As a fair sample of
the verse, the following lines are taken from page 30:

> Such were our themes, when *Fingal* lov'd to hear
> The harp sweet-sounding in his list'ning ear;
> When, at his call, the bards their songs did raise,
> And told the moving tales of former days:
> When from the hills the chiefs, all gathering round,
> Wrapt in attention, heard th' affecting sound.
> First of a thousand bards in *Cona* fam'd,
> Then was my voice, *the voice of* Cona nam'd.
> Great my renown, while yet in youth I sung;
> But now harsh discord has untun'd my tongue!

At the very time when many poets were thus engaged in turning *Ossian* into verse, various other
writers began imitating the rhythmic cadences of

---

[1] The *Annual Register*, 1761, p. 276.

Macpherson's artificial prose. And indeed our literature owes to Macpherson perhaps the major part in establishing "measured prose" as a popular form. From the rhapsody *On the Birth of a Prince, in Imitation of Ossian*, by T. Potts, I have chosen enough extracts to show an eighteenth-century hybrid not very different from our modern free verse:

And did I not hear the voice of joy, the song of the harp in the hall of shells! It comes to the roar of war as the breeze along the heath, when the traveller sweats in his midday-toil. . . . The chiefs sat around the king, his countenance of youth was pensive; for painful is the dread of hope; an awful gloom was around, and silence dwellt in the hall. . . . The renown of heroes is given to the song, but the song of the bards is oft forgot, and the voice of grey hairs is oft feeble; but thou, O king of the white-cliff'd isle! thou shalt live in the glory of thy race, and thy sons shall ever be foremost amid the throng of heroes.

Meanwhile Ferdinando Warner, in a scholarly little pamphlet drawing freely on Keating's *History of Ireland* and Flaherty's *Ogygia*, pointed out that Fingal was really of Irish, rather than Scottish, origin.[1] But in spite of the doubt cast on Macpherson's integrity as translator and editor by Warner and a host of others, Ossian was ready for his debut on the Edinburgh stage.

[1] *Remarks on the History of Fingal, and Other Poems of Ossian* (London, 1762).

The author who undertook the interesting task of dramatizing *Ossian*, David Erskine Baker,[1] evidently felt the English text too sacred to tamper with; adding only the necessary stage directions, he published *The Muse of Ossian: A Dramatic Poem of Three Acts, Selected from the Several Poems of Ossian the Son of Fingal. As it is Performed at the Theatre in Edinburgh.* (Edinburgh, 1763.)[2] In view of the almost inevitable lack of unity, one is not surprised to see in the copy at the British Museum the brief MS. comment: "The Muse of Ossian is a vile Scottish jade." A fairer criticism was to come from the *Monthly Review* of September:

The intention of the Compiler of this piece being to restore an ancient Bard to the still more universal observation of the world in general, and his own country in particular, we are told, he hath laid down as a fundamental point, to avoid as much as possible the blending any base alloy of his own, with the sterling poetry of the immortal Ossian: and, by only connecting some few of the principal incidents of the different songs, to form one little uniform drama, in which the several characters should constantly speak the language of the Bard, and appear, as near as possible, what he himself intended they should be. The Reader will find, that Mr. Baker hath not ill-executed his design; although

[1] For a short biography of Baker, see the *European Magazine* for February, 1782, p. 112.

[2] A notice of publication appears in the *Scots Magazine* for April, 1763, p. 218.

we cannot imagine his compilement would have any
very pleasing effect on the stage.

Meanwhile the Ossianic controversy continued to
rage, and the Celts got a good deal of gratuitous
advertising. *Fingal King of Morven, A Knight-
Errant* (London, 1764), an anonymous criticism,
attempted in forty-seven pages to show that the
characters of Macpherson's *Ossian* were relatively
modern — that in ascribing them to the third
century, Macpherson had erred by at least a thousand years.

After this sort of argument over *Ossian* had been
advanced, refuted, and reiterated, William Julius
Mickle ventured in 1767 to produce a vaguely Celtic
piece, *The Concubine, a Poem in the Manner of Spen-
ser*. A second edition appeared in 1769, and a third
in 1776 — this time with the title changed to *Sir
Martyn*. One of the chief characters of the poem is
the "Wizard," who seems to be Druidical. Mention
is made of Cadwal and "Trojan Brute," and the
setting of the story is Cambria. Like many later
poets, Mickle used a little Celtic material to give a
touch of mystery. "I was aware," he wrote to Lord
Lyttleton about one of his poems, "that the religion
of the Druids was in many instances very different
from what I had used." [1]

In 1768 an operatic arrangement of *Ossian* was
produced on the London stage, with music by F. H.

---

[1] *Poems* (London, 1794), p. xxviii.

Barthelemon. The title of the published work is *Oithóna,*[1] *a dramatic poem, taken from the prose translation of the Celebrated Ossian. As performed at the Theatre Royal in Hay Market. Set to Music by Mr. Barthelemon* (London, 1758). The plot is interesting and contains enough action, as may be seen from the following synopsis, to hold the attention of an audience. In Act I, Gaul, in a dream, finds that his beloved Oithóna has been carried off by Dunrommath, Chief of Cuthal, to his cave in the Island of Tromáthon. In Act II, Gaul finds Oithóna on the island and hears from her lips the details of her capture. Act III contains the battle between Gaul and the Chief of Cuthal, in which the latter is slain along with ten of his followers. After his victory Gaul finds a wounded youth, who turns out to be Oithóna in disguise, seeking death after her shame. Amid much lamentation Oithóna dies, and the opera ends.

Among the enthusiasts who thought *Ossian* would appear better in verse was John Wodrow. *Carthon, The Death of Cuchullin, and Dar-thula: Poems, By Ossian the Son of Fingal. Attempted in English Verse, from Mr. Macpherson's Translation* (Edinburgh, 1769) is the first, though by no means

---

[1] The opera *Oithóna* has apparently been confused by some critics with Alexander Dow's *Sethona* (see Schnabel's misleading statement in *Englische Studien,* XXIII, pp. 45–46). But *Sethona* is wholly Egyptian.

the most pretentious, of Wodrow's testimonials to
his faith in Macpherson. The poems appear here in
very fair heroic couplets.

In 1769 John Home, the famous author of *Douglas*, took from *Ossian* the names, the imagery, and
much of the plot of his *Fatal Discovery*. Elaborating
the story of Ronnan, Connan, and Rivine, suggested
in the ninth of Macpherson's *Fragments*, Home
built up a blank verse tragedy of five acts with some
good dramatic situations. The style, I should judge,
is too affectedly Ossianic to be always free from
obscurity on the stage. If we may believe the following account of the real reason for the failure of
the play, it is one of the clearest examples of the
way in which popular prejudice against the Scots
retarded the progress of the Celtic Revival.

In 1769, his tragedy of *The Fatal Discovery* was
brought out at Drury-Lane. Its original title was
Rivine, from the name of the heroine of the story, which
was taken from one of the fragments of Ossian. But
Garrick, afraid of the prejudices then prevalent in London against Scotsmen, and Scots subjects, changed its
name to that of the Fatal Discovery; and, in order
more effectively to disguise its origin, procured a young
English gentleman, a student from Oxford, to attend
the rehearsals, and personate the author. But the success of the play drew its real author from the covert;
and after some nights' representation, Mr. Home de-
clared himself the writer of the tragedy. The event
verified the fears of Garrick; the succeeding representa-

tions were but indifferently attended, and the piece languished only for a few nights longer.[1]

While William Duff had scarcely mentioned Ossian in his *Essay on Original Genius* (1767), he came in the course of a few years to hold a very high opinion of the Celtic bard — so high that in 1770 he published his *Critical Observations on the Writings of the most celebrated original Geniuses in Poetry, being a Sequel to the Essay on Original Genius.* Here we find the second section of the sequel devoted to a eulogy of Ossian, with the confident assertion that only three "*compleat* original geniuses" had arisen in the world — Homer, Ossian, and Shakespeare; and of these Duff seems inclined to give the palm to Ossian.[2]

Still another item is worth noting, in that it praises Ossian, this time in verse. J. Tait devoted the second stanza of his *Bards of Scotland: An Elegy* to this tribute:

> Bless'd be the isle where Ossian rais'd the song!
> As nature taught him in fair Fancy's grove;
> Whose Muse could thunder with the warlike throng,
> Or melt the soul with softest tales of love.[3]

[1] *The Works of John Home, Esq., Now First Collected. To which is Prefixed an Account of his Life and Writings*, by Henry Mackenzie (Edinburgh, 1822), 1, pp. 62–63.

[2] While I have not been able to find a copy of the sequel in the British Museum or elsewhere, there is fortunately a very full review in the *Gentleman's Magazine*, July, 1770, pp. 32–66.

[3] From the *Scots Magazine*, 1770, p. 617.

MINOR SYMPTOMS OF INTEREST IN THE
CELTS, 1760–1770

In addition to the Celtic-English poems and plays
already listed, the years 1760–1770 showed numerous traces of Celtic interest, not very important
individually, but of significance as a group. It may
suffice to list them chronologically, with very brief
comment.

1760. J. B. B. d'Anville, *Notice de l'ancienne
Gaule, tirée des monumens Romains* (Paris, 1760);
pp. xxvi + 754. An alphabetically arranged geog-
raphy of Gaul, giving the latitude and longitude
of each place and the facts reported about it by
various Latin writers. (Important for this study
because a copy was in the library of the poet Gray.[1])

James Foot wrote *Penseroso*, published 1771, containing important Celtic material discussed below,
pages 106 ff.

1761. Confusion between Celtic and Teutonic
was still so common that the *Annual Register* (pp.
236–237) could print "Fragments of Celtic poetry,
from Olaus Verelius, a German writer," as a title to
The Incantation of Hervor.

Evan Evans began his correspondence with
Bishop Percy. (See above, pp. 27, 28, 42, and 43.)

Samuel Derrick, *Connal and Crimora*, in good

[1] See above, p. 37.

heroic couplets (*Scots Magazine*, Feb., 1761, p. 95), from *Ossian*.

An anonymous poem, *To a brother Druid* (*Gentleman's Magazine*, 1761, p. 470). The word *Druid* is used as a synonym for *poet*.

Occasional Thoughts On the Study and Character of Classical Authors . . . with some Incidental Comparisons of Homer and Ossian (London, 1762). Anonymous. This is an educational treatise, otherwise sensible, which shows that as early as 1762 a writer not concerned directly in the Ossianic controversy could prefer Ossian to Homer. See especially pages 99 ff.

Gisbal, an Hyperborean Tale: Translated from the Fragments of Ossian the Son of Fingal. The Second Edition (London, 1762). An anonymous satire on *Ossian*, with apparently a political aim.

An Elegy on Major Alexander MacLean. In imitation of Ossian. (*Scots Magazine*, 1762, p. 604.) A prose poem by "Montanus," showing indirectly how much *Ossian* was revered, and its peculiar style admired.

1763. Michael Wodhull, *To the Dryads* (Oxford, 1763). Stanza eleven contains a digression on the cruelty of human sacrifice among the Druids.

Bonnel Thornton satirized the revival of interest in "Antient British Musick" in his burlesque *Ode on St. Cecelia's Day*, performed at Ranelagh to a crowded house on June 10. The satire is so clever that Edward Jones included it in his *Musical and Poetical Relicks of the Welsh Bards*.

Samuel Derrick, *The Battle of Lora, a Poem, with some Fragments written in the Erse or Irish Language by Ossian, the Son of Fingal, translated into English verse by Mr. Derrick* (London, 1763).

1764. Rowland Jones of Broom Hall, *The Origin of Language and Nations* (London, 1765). Contains a valuable bibliography after the Preface; also a Celtic grammar, a Comparative Etymological Lexicon of the English, Welsh, Greek, and Latin languages, etc. The first of six amazing volumes by Jones, which cannot be taken seriously to-day.

1765. *Ode to the Lyric Muse* (*Scots Magazine*, Feb., 1765, pp. 101–102). An anonymous poem of which the seventh stanza treats the Druidical Bards.

Bishop Percy, in his *Reliques*, reprinted *Winifreda*, which he took from David Lewis's *Miscellaneous Poems by Various Hands* (1726). "It is there said, how truly I know not, to be ' a translation from the ancient British language.' "

1766. Henry Rowlands, *Mona Antiqua Restaurata*, second edition (London, 1766), revised by Henry Owen and the great Welsh antiquary, Lewis Morris; supplemented by *A History of the Island of Anglesey, by Nicholas Owen*. As Rowlands died before the proof of the first edition (Dublin, 1723) was corrected, this is the definitive edition. It was widely used by Celtic-English poets for information about the Druids. Richard Lluyd, Bard of Snowdon, referred to it so often in the notes to his *Beaumaris Bay* that on page 21 he called it "Rowland's M. A."

1768. Thomas Gray, *Owen*. Important English rendering of Welsh poetry, already mentioned in Chapter III, pages 48 ff.

1770. Johann Ewald, *Rolf Krage* (Copenhagen, 1770), a tragedy, in Danish, showing strong influence from *Ossian*.[1]

From a study of the years 1760–1770 it is evident that they were by no means rich in Celtic-English poetry. Most of the pieces produced were mere adaptations or imitations of Macpherson's *Ossian*, and the genuine Celtic material was thus twice adulterated before it was ready for English consumption. Nevertheless, the public became increasingly interested in Celtic mythology and Druidism, so that it was better prepared to appreciate the more meritorious productions of the decades immediately following.

[1] See *Dansk Biografisk Lexikon utgivet af C. F. Bricka*, IV, p. 632. Ewald learned English so as to be able to read Shakespeare and Macpherson's *Ossian* without a translation.

CHAPTER VI

1771-1780

IN 1771, John Wodrow, apparently encouraged by the success of his metrical versions of *Carthon*, *The Death of Cuchullin*, and *Darthula*, published in two pretentious volumes *Fingal, an ancient epic poem. In six books. By Ossian the son of Fingal. Translated into English heroic rhyme, by John Wodrow, M.A., one of the Ministers of Islay* (Edinburgh, 1771). One of the amazing features is the Preface of a hundred pages, with its long quotations from Hugh Blair's *Dissertation*. Of Wodrow's whole-souled belief in the honesty of Macpherson's work some idea is given by the opening sentence:

> To entertain any doubt of the antiquity or authenticity of the poems of Ossian, as some pretend to do, can flow only from an affected singularity of thinking, or from the mere wantonness of prejudice.

In the same year James Foot published his *Penseroso, or the Pensive Philosopher in his Solitudes, a Poem in six books* (London, 1771). This is a long didactic treatise written under the influence of "the elegant Mr. Mason," whom the author mentions in the Preface. As a note on page 251 informs us that the last part of *Penseroso* was written "in the be-

ginning of the year 1760," it is fairly safe to assume
that the author's attention had been called to
Druidism by Mason's *Caractacus*, of which two
editions had appeared in 1759. Of the portion of the
poem dealing with Druidism, it seems that the following passage from Book IV (beginning on page
161) shows the influence of Mason:

> High on this hill, and down yon craggy steep
> Delv'd into caves, wide-spreading rose the oaks
> Gloomy as night, the consecrated haunt
> Of ancient Druids: on each father tree,
> Each father tree a wood, so broad his arms,
> Fair hung the Mistletoe like burnish'd gold
> Of mystic pow'r, and glitter'd through the shade.
> Deep-scoop'd and shagg'd with boughs yon ran the cave
> Beneath the mountain's brow, where dark-immur'd
> And held a God, the Seer of Druids liv'd,
> His white-rob'd brotherhood in neighbouring shades
> At awful distance seated.

It is not without interest to note that Foot, writing
so early in the Celtic Revival, felt called on to explain
his reference to Druidism in the following note:

Of the Druids there were three orders, the Druids
properly so called, the Euvates, and the Bardi. It is
very certain that they dealt in human sacrifices, and
believed the doctrines of the conflagration [*sic*] and the
transmigration of souls. They are supposed to have
derived their religion from the Magi. Those of Britain
were the most celebrated for their learning, and for the
great respect and honour which they received from the
world. The accounts we have of them from history are

very short, being almost lost in the wilds of time. It is
certain also, that they taught some great and useful
truths; but whether they addicted themselves to all
the idolatry and superstition of the other Gentiles, is
not here determined. The intent of this book is to expose the wickedness and folly of idolatry in general, but
not that merely of the Druids in particular; and a
liberty is herein assumed of imbellishing this account
of the matter, with such circumstances as are in part
true from history, and partly probable. (Page 198.)

Apparently the public was becoming thoroughly
aroused to the possibilities of Celtic-English poetry,
for only a year after Wodrow's *Fingal* we find *Fingal, a poem in six books by Ossian: Translated from
the original Galic by Mr. Macpherson, and Rendered
into Verse from that Translation* [By Richard Hole]
(Oxford, 1772).[1] Hole's *Fingal* has a sensible Preface, followed by an *Ode to Imagination*, which de-
scribes the Kingdom of Morven as the author,
guided by imagination, sees it. Then come the six
books of *Fingal* in heroic couplets.

As a pleasant change from these revampings of
Macpherson's work, came George Edmund Howard's tragedy, *The Siege of Tamor*, first published at
Dublin in 1773 and twice reprinted at London in the
same year. "For the story on which this Tragedy is

[1] That this anonymous rendering was by Richard Hole, and not by
Hoole, as Schnabel and others have conjectured, I have established
in a short contribution to *Modern Language Notes*.

formed," says the author, "see Doctor Warner's History of Ireland . . . also Keating's Antiquities thereof." From start to finish it is a drama of war and blood, the lyric element being almost negligible. The plot turns on the victory of the Irish over the Danes who invaded Ireland in the ninth century; and a romantic tone is given by the love of Niall, King of Ulster, for Eernestha, daughter of the King of Leinster. Howard shows no influence from Macpherson, or, so far as I can see, from Mason; his idea of the manners, customs, and religions of the Celts and the Danes was gained from a careful study of the well-known treatises by O'Connor, Keating, Warner, and Mallet, to whom he expresses his indebtedness. Of special interest is Act IV, Scene 4, where Malsechlin offers to sacrifice his daughter to propitiate the gods.

Another poet, James Graeme, was among the precursors of the Romantic movement in his warm admiration of "the Gothic, Celtic, and Oriental mythology." [1] His *Rona* shows obvious influence from Macpherson, but is unusual in its freedom from the conventional heroic couplets of the day. A brief quotation will illustrate his style:

> How fell the hero? In his might,
> Amid his growing fame!
> Not feeble was Hildallan's foe,
> His sword a meteor's flame.

[1] See Robert Anderson's *Poets of Great Britain* (1794), XI.

No more shall Morna's hall rejoice,
The feast of shells be spread;
The sigh of Rona's secret soul
In Death's dark house is laid.[1]

In Thomas Mercer's volume entitled *Poems. By
the Author of the Sentimental Sailor* (Edinburgh,
1774) are two pieces of some significance. The first,
Arthur's Seat, a description of the beauties of Scottish scenery, has a footnote showing a remarkable
combination in the author's mind of influences from
Arthurian romances and Macpherson's *Ossian*:

The vulgar tradition, that Arthur's Seat originates
from a British prince or chief of that name viewing a
battle from the top of it, may not perhaps be altogether so fabulous as our antiquaries have generally
supposed. For that such was the custom of the ancient
inhabitants of this island, is evident from the poems of
Ossian. [In support of this assertion, Mercer quotes
the following passage from Macpherson]: "My sword
shall wave on that hill, and be the shield of my people.
— High on Cromla's side he sat, waving the lightning of
his sword, and as he waved we moved. Fingal, b. 4."

The second poem in this collection, *Elysium: A
Dream*, a daring imitation of the sixth book of the
Æneid, shows the author amid the Elysian fields,
meeting in succession Homer and Ossian: [2]

---

[1] The whole poem may be found in *Poems on Several Occasions* by
James Graeme (Edinburgh, 1773).

[2] That James Barry, R. A., included Ossian among the celebrities
in his picture "Elizium" has been pointed out to me by Professor

In hoary majesty sublime,
Triumphant o'er the waste of Time,
Who, bending, sweeps the Celtic lyre?
Who tears the soul, or burns with fire?

"O! by the wild, tumultuous jar
Of battle wag'd in glorious war;
The gen'rous deed; the prostrate foe;
Th' arrested sword; the sigh of woe!

By livid ghost, on fiery stream
Descending, sad, in warrior's dream,
With airy sword, and meteor shield,
That fatal speaks the future field!

By chiding Cona's solemn sound;
The drooping flower; the sallow [fallow?] ground;
The falling leaf that trembling flies;
The blasted pine that broken lies;
O! by the hero's narrow cell!
Sing, pensive bard, thy last farewell!"   [Pp. 85–86.]

During the winter of 1774–1775, John Abraham
Fisher's *Masque of the Druids* was successfully performed at Covent Garden on various days, with a

Tinker. Barry says in his *Account of a Series of Pictures, in the Great
Room. . . . at the Adelphi* (London, 1783), pp. 135–136: "Behind Sappho,
who is near Chaucer . . . sits the poet Alceus, who was so much
admired by the ancients, though his writings are lost, yet fortunately
there is a head of him remaining, and from the noble and spirited account Horace gives of his abilities, I have found a companion for him,
very much of his own cast, in our ancient bard Ossian, with whom he
is talking." After discussing briefly the Ossianic question, Barry says
further: "I agree, however, with the learned and very ingenuous
[*sic*] Mr. Shaw, that Ossian, whatever his abilities may have been as
a bard, was an Irish bard . . . I have accordingly given Ossian the
Irish harp, and the lank black hair, and open unreserved countenance, peculiar to his native country."

total of at least ten performances.[1] The extant
score [London, 1774], shows that Druids were represented on the stage. The "First Druid" begins his
song thus:

> Holy Druids,
> From your consecrated woods,
> Rocks, cliffs, and silver floods,
> From their margins fring'd with flowers,
> Hither move; forsake your bow'rs,
> Strew'd with hallow'd oaken leaves,
> Deck'd with flags and sedgy sheaves.
> To yon bright dome now straight repair,
> But leave behind you all your care.

Once more we must record a metrical version of
Fingal, this being perhaps the most pretentious of
all, by Ewen Cameron: *The Fingal of Ossian . . .
Now Rendered into English Heroic Verse* (Warrington, 1776).[2] It is an expensive volume of over
five hundred pages large quarto, containing Hugh
Blair's *Attestations*, a long Preface, and the six
books of *Fingal* profusely annotated. The notes,
which are gleanings from the writings of Macpherson and many of his followers, seem absurd in the
light of more recent researches; but in them was the
chief value to the eighteenth century of Cameron's
work. The versification is miserable, and that it
was so regarded by the poet's contemporaries is

---

[1] See the Theatrical Register in the *Gentleman's Magazine*, January, 1775, p. 45; also Baker's *Biog. Dramat.*
[2] The title page was changed in 1777 to read "London, 1777."

shown by an incisive review in the *Critical* for March, 1777.

In the *Relicques of Genius* (London, 1777) appeared Everhard Ryan's ode, *Uther and the Son of Owen*, containing various Celtic proper names and a trace of the morbid melancholy characteristic of *Ossian*. The poem is singularly lacking in action, but we are indirectly led to understand that the Son of Owen is killed by Uther, a rival for the hand of Bela. The last of the six stanzas runs thus:

> Soft from the hill, what voice of woe
> Pours on the gale the plaintive strain?
> Thy tears, afflicted maiden, flow,
> Washing thy lovely cheek in vain.
> Long shall the breezes waft thy mournful sighs,
> Bleeding and pale the son of Owen lies.

John Ogilvie's *Rona, a Poem, in Seven Books* (London, 1777) begins with an invocation to Ossian: [1]

> O thou, who, wrapt in night's involving gloom,
> Sang of the gliding ghost and lonely tomb;
> Of beauty stretch'd in dust, of hosts o'erthrown [etc.].

Similarly, the opening lines of Book VII are a tribute to Ossian:

> Hark! — From th' Æolian lute yon sounds of woe!
> How wildly-sweet yon dying numbers flow!
> Dim o'er the strings what aery fingers stray!
> Ah! what soft breath prolongs that trembling lay!

[1] For the fact that these lines are to Ossian, see the Introduction, p. xv.

> I feel the quiv'ring note! — Some Angel near
> Slow waves the stream on this delighted ear!
> Or he the Bard, whose deeply-plaintive lyre,
> When gliding phantoms skimm'd its warbling wire,
> Wailed through the night.* . . .

These lines show something of Ogilvie's poetic ability, which he was to put to better use ten years later in *The Fane of the Druids*.

In 1778 appeared *The Works of Hugh Kelly* (London), containing a Macphersonian poem entitled *Crimora: An Elegy. Translated from the Erse, with some Alterations.* The fifteen stanzas of melancholy may be adequately represented by the first:

> Pale horror now, through each secluded cave,
>   A dreary refuge from the tempest finds;
> The distant murmur of the faltering wave,
>   Sinks on the panting bosom of the wind.

Henry Brooke, who was much interested in Celtic literature, produced at least three pieces showing striking Celtic touches. We are told that "he resolved to learn the Irish language, a resolve, with many others, which he never put into execution. A person, whose name is now forgotten, furnished him with a literal translation of many of the most popular poems in that tongue." [1] By far the most

---

* In the beautiful poem called *Berrathon*. — "My harp" (says *Ossian*) "hangs on a blasted branch. The sound of its strings is mournful. — Does the wind touch thee, O harp! or is it some passing ghost? — It is the hand of Malvina!" [Ogilvie's note.]

[1] From *Brookiana*, by C. H. W. (London, 1804), I, pp. 86–87.

interesting of his works is the drama *Cymbeline*, with its effective Celtic mythology and Druidism.[1] Scenes 4–10, inclusive, of Act V are laid in the temple of the goddess Andate. A quotation and summary will show the excellent use Brooke makes of his Druidical rites to give vividness and action to the play:

SCENE IV

Opens and discovers the inside of the Temple; the Altar of Incense, with the sacred fire, and the Altar of Sacrifice. The Choir and sacred Music at the upper end. The Priests ranged on either hand; a Roman victim standing behind each Priest, with his hands bound, and adorned with ribbons and garlands.

Priestess. Begin your dread solemnities.
(*Symphony of Music, and the Hymn sung by Priests and Priestesses*)

HYMN

I

Goddess of conflicting arms,
Of the field and of the fight,
Brazen sounds, and dread alarms,
Conquest, slaughter, fear, and flight!

---

[1] Note that Brooke wrote the Epilogue to Howard's *Siege of Tamor* (see above, p. 108), as well as a long fragmentary poem, *Conrade*, showing traces of influence from Macpherson. See *A Collection of the Pieces Formerly Published by Henry Brooke, Esq. to which are added several Plays and Poems Now First Printed* (London, 1778), IV, pp. 394 ff. In 1743 he had (according to the D. N. B.) issued the prospectus of a collection of "Ogygian Tales; or a curious Collection of Irish Fables, Allegories, and Histories," but there was not enough interest in the subject to warrant publication. A similar fate awaited the history of Ireland which Brooke projected in 1744.

II

To thee, triumphant, potent maid,
Be our vows and offerings paid!
Should domestic guilt displease,
Hostile blood shall best appease.

Priestess. List now — Thus saith our ancient oracle:
When a victim, free to live,
Shall his life for others give —
Human offerings shall, no more,
Stain the land with human gore.

So says the sentence of two thousand years —
But, no such victim comes!
Ye know your duty.

(*To the Priests — each of whom seizes his Captive and draws a
poniard, ready to strike*)

Immediately after this we have the entrance of
Leonatus, who, being tired of life, offers himself as a
voluntary sacrifice. After some dialogue, he is
bound and laid on the altar, while the Priests and
Priestesses chant verses beginning:

Not in malice, but in love,
Dress him as a feast for Jove.

(This may astonish the reader, who recollects that
the sacrifice was intended not for Jove, but Andate!)
Just as the bowl is ready to receive his blood, there
is a crash of thunder, and the sacred fire is extin-
guished. As this is taken as a sign of divine dis-
approval, the sacrifice is delayed, and Leonatus
becomes engaged in conversation with the Priest.
Only then is it discovered that Leonatus is himself

the son of the Priest. From this point the dénoue-
ment proceeds rapidly.[1]

The first follower of Macpherson who made an
effort to forge a considerable number of Gaelic
poems, and to pass them off on the public as genuine,
was John Clark, who in 1778 published a small
volume called *Works of the Caledonian Bards.
Translated from the Galic. Volume I.* (Edinburgh.)
Although no second volume ever appeared, a second
edition of this one was issued in 1783. Of all the
attempts to hoodwink the reading public, this is
among the most brazen. Anyone with the slightest
knowledge of Gaelic can see at a glance that the
work is a forgery; indeed, it seems impossible that
so many pages of notes could have been written
without including at least a few more correct statements. For instance, the "translator" is commenting on *deud gealdh*, well-known Gaelic words
for *teeth* and *white*, by which they are perfectly
rendered into English, *deud* being an actual cognate
of *tooth*. In defense of his translation "white formers
of the ivory ring," he says:

What is here translated, *white formers of the ivory ring*,
stands in the original, *Deud Gealdh*; a term to which no

[1] The play was published, probably for the first time, in Brooke's
Collection, cited in the previous note, vol. III, pp. 169 ff. Of course the
Cymbeline story was always popular in the drama, *Shakespeare's* version having been altered by Thomas D'Urfey and by William Haw-
kins; but apparently Brooke was the first to reproduce in such detail
the religious rites of the Druids.

word in the English language bears the smallest affinity. When such terms occur, the translation must undoubtedly lose all the beauties of the original.

Deud signifies a graceful assemblage of refined objects, whose perfections astonish the beholders, and excite the most agreeable sensations; a term applied by the Celtic bards to the fine set teeth of the ladies.

A few remarks on this passage will contribute to support the truth of an assertion, which the translator has formerly presumed to advance; That the Galic, even in its present uncultivated state, displays a luxuriant richness of poetical terms, incomparably superior to any of the modern languages. The care which the ladies of our days take to have the avenue leading to their gentle stomachs adorned with a proper set of ivory sentinels, leaves no room to doubt, but these champions do great execution in the day of battle. A troop, which has so often distinguished itself in the cause of the fair, ought then by no means to be forgot, when the triumphs of their victories are rehearsing; yet poetry, which pretends to do justice to every member and minute feature of the victorious beauty, has, with an unpardonable negligence, suffered the teeth to sleep without their fame, while the actions of the eyes, lips, chin, etc., are magnified by repeated eulogiums. [Etc., etc. I have quoted only the first half of the note, pp. 169–170.]

The most pretentious piece in the collection, *Morduth, an Antient Heroic Poem in Three Books,* is in a prose form which utterly fails to reproduce the "measured" effect achieved by Macpherson. The whole production is literally as absurd as the note already quoted; an unusually intelligent passage may be given as a specimen:

The departure of the pale-faced son of night was on the wings of the sudden blast. Oaks of strength trembled before the haste of his retiring steps. The groans of woods were heard, as he rushed on the clouds of his speed through their whistling locks. [Pages 42–43.]

Most of the "translations" are as insipid as this, except *The Antient Chief*, which purports to be by a contemporary Highland bard, and is given in tolerable heroic couplets. The ignorance of the critics of the day is well illustrated by the fact that neither the *Critical Review* [1] nor the *Monthly Review* [2] expressed any serious doubt as to the genuineness of the collection.

The two volumes of Thomas Pennant's *Tours in Wales* illustrate very well the headway gained by the Celtic Revival towards the close of the seventh decade.[3] They are replete with interesting and conservative comments on the antiquities of Celtic Britain, and on the religion and mythology of the ancient inhabitants. On pages 281 ff. of the first

[1] See the issue for July, 1778, for favorable criticism, quoting the poem *Comala and Orwi*.

[2] See the issue for November, 1778, for a letter of commendation.

[3] Vol. I was published at London in 1778, Vol. II in 1781; but for the sake of coherence it will be well to discuss them together.

volume is Richard Williams's *Ode to Myfanwy
Vechan*, of which the original Welsh, by Howel ap
Einion Lygliw, had been printed in Evan Evans's
Specimens of the Poetry of the Antient Welsh Bards
(pp. 115–118), and the English prose in the same
volume (pp. 14–16). As a sample I quote the last
eight lines:

> O, fairer than the flowers adorning
> The hawthorn in a summer's morning!
> While life remains, I still will sing
> Thy praise, and make the mountains ring
> With fair Myfanwy's tuneful name!
> And from misfortune purchase fame;
> Nor ev'n to die shall I repine,
> So Howel's name shall live with thine.

An English metrical version of Taliesin's poem,
Elphin's Consolation, likewise of genuine Welsh
origin,[1] is said by Pennant to have been written by
"a fair countrywoman of mine and printed in 1780,
4to, and sold by Dodsley and Elmsley." The following is an extract from the third stanza:

> Though like a slender reed I grow,
> Toss'd by the billows to and fro,
> Yet still, by Him inspir'd, my song
> The weak can raise, confound the strong:
> Am I not better, Elphin, say,
> Than thousands of thy scaly prey?

Passing over the fifteen irregular stanzas of the

---

[1] See Pennant, II, 148 ff. For the original Welsh, see Evans's
Specimens, pp. 150–151; for the English prose, pp. 56–57.

Hirlas Owain,[1] we come to a beautiful piece, also by Williams, *The Favorite of Gwalchmai*,[2] which may be quoted entire.

> Rise, Orb of Day! the eastern gates unfold,
> And shew thy crimson mantle fring'd with gold.
> Contending birds sing sweet on ev'ry spray;
> The skies are bright; — arise thou Orb of Day!
> I, Gwalchmai, call; in song, in war renown'd,
> Who Lion-like, confusion spread around.
> The live-long night, the Hero and the Bard
> Near Freiddin's rocks have kept a constant guard;
> Where cool transparent streams in murmurs glide,
> And springing grass adorns the mountain's side;
> Where snow-white sea-mews in the current play,
> Spread their gay plumes, and frolic through the day.

Of considerable interest as an example of the identification of the Celtic spirit with the spirit of liberty, is the poem by Sneyd Davis, also included by Pennant. The hero of the poem, Caractacus, is here praised to the skies, and then begged to inspire the modern Britons to further deeds of valor against the French.

That the poets were gradually coming to know more about Druidism is again illustrated by some lines, with an explanatory note, in Robert Holmes's *Alfred* (Oxford, 1778):

---

[1] Page 288; by Richard Williams, from Evans's *Specimens*, pp. 7–13.

[2] Here again the Welsh original is in Evans's *Specimens*, p. 83; a Latin translation, p. 84. Evans gives no English version.

> No more th' impenetrable groves among,
> With sacred spoils and idol-trophies hung,
> From altars foul dark wreaths of smoke
> Imbosom the religious Oak;
> When rous'd by Mona's bloody-mantled Priest.*
> Impatient Homicide, his Druid-crew
> With eyes of madness watch the midnight spell,
> And drown with deaf'ning yell
> The scream of Captives stretch'd in furnace blue.

A year after the appearance of *Alfred*, a more noticeably Celtic piece was published in the anonymous volume, *Poetical Effusions. To which is added, The War of Inis-Thona; a Poem, from Ossian, in English verse* (London, 1779). The Argument of *The War of Inis-Thona* is as follows:

REFLECTIONS of *Ossian* on his youth. An apostrophe to *Selma*. *Oscar* his Son obtains leave to go to *Inis-Thona*, an island of *Scandinavia*. The mournful story of *Argon* and *Ruro*, the two Sons of the King of *Inis-Thona*. *Oscar* revenges their death, and returns in triumph to *Selma*. A Soliloquy by the Poet.

A great number of different verse-forms are employed, with, on the whole, a pleasing effect. As a sample I quote the last few lines:

* The Island of Mona, which now bears the name of Anglesey, was antiently sacred to the superstition of the Druids. Cæsar informs us, that they had a Chief or Head, to whom they gave sovereign power. They paid particular veneration to the Oak, and usually solemnized their religious rites in the deepest recesses of the forests. Their human sacrifices were forbidden by Augustus and Tiberius, and abolished by Claudius. Sueton. in Vit. Claudii. [Holmes's note.]

Yes, like him, renown'd in story,
Morven's Sons shall have their glory;
Oft the songs my bosom chear,
My youthful Friends remember'd dear.
Gentle sleep my sense decoys
With the harp's descending joys:
Dreams of pleasure now arise,
Former days enchant my eyes.
Sons of the Chace, Oh! come not near,
Reclin'd while Ossian slumbers here;
For the Bard delights to hold
Converse with the Chiefs of old:
Sons of the jocund Chace, Oh! come not near,
Nor break his happy dreams while Ossian slumbers here.

In 1780 the *Annual Register* printed Christopher Butson's poem, *On the Love of Our Country*, which had won the Chancellor's Prize at Oxford. The poem is of some interest for its happy combination of patriotism and liberty with Celtic history and Druidism.[1]

In the same year John Smith published at Edinburgh his *Galic Antiquities*. Part I, *The History of the Druids*, is thoroughly unreliable; Part II, a dissertation attempting to support the authenticity of Macpherson's *Ossian*, is all wrong; Part III, a collection of thirteen English prose poems said to have been written by Ossian, is a forgery.[2] So far

[1] See the *Annual Register*, 1780, pp. 197–199. Seventeen years later the poem was reprinted in the *Gentleman's Magazine* (1797, pp. 151–152), from which, by a curious oversight, it was copied into the *Annual Register* for the same year.

[2] See L. C. Stern, *Die Ossianischen Heldenlieder*, in Koch's *Zeitschrift*, N. F. VIII, p. 70.

as I have observed, the poems had little effect
on English literature; they abound with a sickly
sentimentalism, and, as Stern justly remarks, "über-
macphersonieren Macpherson."[1] After seven years
Smith had composed his "originals" in Gaelic,
which he published under the title of *Sean Dana;
le Oisian, Ullan, &c. Ancient Poems of Ossian, Ullin,
&c. Collected in the Western Highlands and Isles;
Being the Originals of the Translations some time ago
Published in the Gaelic* [sic] *Antiquities* (Edinburgh,
1787).

MINOR SYMPTOMS OF INTEREST IN THE CELTS, 1771–1780

Throughout these ten years there were, as in the
previous decade, numerous manifestations of interest in the Celtic Revival, of just enough importance to be included in this study with the briefest
possible mention.

1771. Dr. John Smith explained in great detail
the Druidical rites which he believed were connected with Stonehenge, in a volume: *Choir Gaur;
The Grand Orrery of the Ancient Druids, Commonly
called Stonehenge, on Salisbury Plain, Astronom-
ically explained, and Mathematically proved to be a
Temple erected in the earliest Ages, for observing the*

---

[1] The titles are: *Gaul, Duthona, Dermid, Finan and Lorma, Cath-
luina, Manos, Trathal, Dargo, Cuthon, The Fall of Tura, Cathlava,* and
The Death of Artho.

Motions of the Heavenly Bodies. . . . By Dr. John Smith, Inoculator of the Smallpox. (Salisbury, 1771.) [Valuable bibliography of works on Stonehenge.]

In Samuel Foote's *Maid of Bath*, Lady Catherine Coldstream calls herself "a lady lineally descended from the great Ossian himself." [1]

The Gwyneddigion Society was formed, by natives of North Wales resident in London, to promote the study of Welsh literature and music. Under its auspices numerous *eisteddfodau* (bardic contests) were subsequently held.[2]

1772. In the anonymous *Ode on British Freedom*, printed on pages 207 ff. of *The Shamrock: or Hibernian Cresses* (Dublin, 1772), the third and fourth stanzas are distinctly Celtic, dealing with Druids, human sacrifice, and battles for freedom, and mentioning the hero Caractacus.

In the same volume, *The Shamrock*, appeared (pp. 340 ff.) a poem of eight irregular stanzas, *The Hone: A Piece of Irish Mythology.*

On March 7 was the first performance at the Théâtre Français, Paris, of Antoine Leblanc de Guillet's tragedy, *Les Druides.*[3]

---

[1] The play was acted in 1771 and published in 1778.

[2] See William Davies Leathart's *Origin and Progress of the Gwyneddigion Society of London* (London, 1831); *The Transactions of the Cymmrodorion Society for 1822*, pp. vii and viii; and Richard Williams in the *Encyclopædia Britannica*, s.v. *Eisteddfod.*

[3] Interesting for being entirely Celtic, but hardly within the scope of the present study. The play was printed at St. Petersburg in 1783.

1773. In April, Francis Dobbs's tragedy, *The Patriot King; or Irish Chief*, was performed at the Smock-Alley Theatre in Dublin.[1] The scene is laid in Dublin at the time when the Irish and the Danes were at war. The hero is Ceallachan, King of Munster; but in other respects the piece is not distinctly Celtic.

There was a brief reference to Ossian in the anonymous poem, *The Origin of Tragedy in Scotland* (printed in the *Scots Magazine*, 1773, p. 42).

John Tait published anonymously *The Cave of Morar*, taking the name *Morar* from *Ossian;* he also published *The Druid's Monument, A Tribute to the Memory of Dr. Oliver Goldsmith* (London, 1774).

The Rev. William Lipscombe published in his *Poems* (Oxford, 1774) an *Ode to Midnight*, containing (ll.77–80) a reference to Druidism.

In General John Burgoyne's fantastic *Maid of the Oaks*, played and printed in 1774, the action is brought to an end by the appearance of "a Druid," who gives his blessing.

John Bennet published in his *Poems* (London, 1774) a piece, *Henry and Rosamund*, in a style slightly suggestive of Macpherson's *Ossian*.

1776. Thomas Maurice made extensive use of early British history in his poem, *Netherby*, and mentioned Druidism on pages 5 and 10.

---

[1] That the play was produced in Dublin at this time is shown by the advertisement of the London edition (1774) and by Genest, X,

1777. Richard Polwhele published anonymously *The Fate of Lewellyn; or, The Druid's Sacrifice. . . . To which is added, The Genius of Carnbre* (Bath, 1777). Both poems contain much Celtic mythology, confused in the first with Norse; but the pieces are too puerile to be valuable. About the same time Polwhele (who was only seventeen years old) wrote *The Cambrian Bards*, published in 1810.

1778. William Tasker published his *Ode to the Warlike Genius of Great Britain* (London, 1778), drawing largely on Celtic mythology and urging the British to resist the threatened invasion from France. The *Ode* was reprinted in Tasker's *Poems* (1779), and in successive issues of the *Gentleman's Magazine* for 1798–1800.

William Pearce made brief mention of Druidism on page 11 of his *Haunts of Shakespeare* (London, 1778).

Hugo Arnot, in his *History of Edinburgh,* gave "a preference to the Druidical over that of the Christian religion," according to J. L. Buchanan's *Defense of the Scots Highlander,* page 252.

1780. In this year it is said that C. Wilson "published a small quarto of Ossianic poetry." [1]

p. 257. Apparently the statement to the contrary in the *D.N.B.* is incorrect.

[1] See Nicholas O'Kearney in *The Battle of Gabhra* (Dublin, printed for the Ossianic Society, 1853), p. 10. I have not found the volume in the British Museum, or any mention of it in the *Gentleman's Magazine* or the *Monthly Review.*

The pieces which have been considered in this chapter show that Celtic influences on English literature were much more pronounced during the eighth decade of the eighteenth century than during the seventh. While Macpherson's unnatural gloom was still reflected in too many poems to suit a more modern and less sentimental taste, there was much independent work of fair quality. The dramatic productions of Howard, Fisher, and Brooke, the recasting into English verse by Williams and others of numerous mediæval bardic poems, three complete metrical versions of *Fingal* — these, together with a great number of short poems on Druidism, combine to make a very respectable body of literature.

CHAPTER VII

1781-1790

AN interesting echo of Gray's *Bard* is to be found
in a passage of Thomas Penrose's poem *The
Harp*, published posthumously in 1781:[1]

> Borne on Fancy's wing along,
>   High soars the bard's enraptur'd soul:
> Round him floats the joy of song,
>   Round him airs extatic roll:
>   Resistless charm! each swelling vein
>   Owns the accustom'd flame, and throbs to pour
>   the strain.
>
> Spirit of Ossian! — thro' the gloom
>   Of ages deepen'd into night,
> See it bursting from the tomb, —
>   O'er it gleams a holy light!
>
>   See! it waves its master-hand;
>   Assembling o'er the heath quick glide the minstrel
>   band.
>   .   .   .   .
>   The list'ning shades, a grisly host,
>   Spring from the narrow cell,
>   And hail with lengthen'd shout th' enchanter's
>   mighty ghost.

[1] Penrose died in 1779. The volume of *Poems* (from which I
quote) was edited by J. P. Andrews. For a favorable review and a
biography of Penrose, see the *European Magazine* for March, 1782,
p. 202. As *The Harp* was not included in Penrose's *Flights of Fancy*
(1775), we may conjecture that it was composed between 1774 and
1780.

Ruthless tyrant, — yield to fate: —
Nor Folly's scorn, nor Rancour's hate,
  Tho' op'ning wide the sluice of gore,
  Could quench the skill divine, could drown the mystic
    lore.

Long! — long indeed 't was mute! thy feeble prey,
Fall'n the hoary minstrels lay: —
  While sick'ning o'er the mournful ground,
  The conquer'd bands oft turn'd the ear in vain.

In the same year appeared Thomas James Mathias's *Runic Odes*, written, like Penrose's *Harp*,
under strong influence from Gray.[1] The word *Runic*
is used by Mathias to include both Celtic and
Scandinavian. The fourth piece in the collection,
Battle, is a striking example of an imitation "from
the works attributed to Ossian," but with a pleasing
freedom from sentimentalism. The next, *Tudor*,
from Evans's *Specimens*, is in nearly as good verse,
and rather more interesting to quote:

ODE V. TUDOR *

Fill the horn of glossy blue,
Ocean's bright caerulean hue;
Briskly quaff the flav'rous mead,
'Tis a day to joy decreed.

[1] In addition to the perfectly evident traces of indebtedness to
Gray in all the *Odes*, it is noteworthy that Mathias edited in 1814 the
great two-volume edition of Gray's *Works* with several MS. essays
never before printed.

* This is not a regular Imitation of any particular Poem in Mr.
Evans's Specimens; but the following Passages, in different parts of

Strike the harp's symphonic string,
Tudor none refuse to sing;
Ne'er shall he belie his birth,
Valour his, and conscious worth.

Have you seen the virgin snow,
That tops old Aran's peering brow;
Or lucid web, by insect spun,
Purpureal gleam in summer sun?
With such, yet far diviner light,
Malvina hits the dazzled sight:
The guerdon such, can Tudor's breast
Dare to court ignoble rest?

From the cliff sublime and hoary
See descending martial glory;
Armed bands aloft uprear
Crimson banner, crimson spear;
Venodotia's ancient boast
Meets the pride of London's host;
On they move with step serene,
And form a dreadly pleasing scene.

Heard you that terrific clang?
Thro' the pathless void it rang:

them, struck me, and occasioned my composing this short mono-
strophic Ode.

"O cup-bearer! fetch the horn that we may drink together, whose
gloss is like the wave of the sea: bring the best meath.

"I have composed with great study and pains, thy praise, O
thou, that shinest like the new-fallen snow of the brow of Aran: —
Thou that shinest like the fine spider's web on the grass in a Summer's
day.

"The army at Offa's dike panted for glory, the troops of Venodotia, and the men of London. —

"He puts numerous troops of his enemies to flight like a mighty
wind." [Mathias's note, p. 33.]

Th' expecting raven screams afar,
And snuffs the reeking spoils of war.
Have you e'er on barren strand
Ta'en your solitary stand,
And seen the whirlwind's spirit sped
O'er the dark green billowy bed?
Glowing in the thickest fight,
Such resistless Tudor's might.

In the same year, 1781, John Pinkerton included in his *Rimes* two Celtic poems, *The Harp of Ossian* and *The Vale of Woe*. The former was so replete with indirect praise of Macpherson that Pinkerton took special pains to cancel it in a later edition, on deciding that Macpherson was a fraud. I quote the opening lines of both poems:

MELODY VI. THE HARP OF OSSIAN

PRELUDE

Tho rich majestic Milton's lay,
Tho ages bend to Homer's sway,
Supreme of Grecian song;
Yet, Ossian, mid the sainted train,
Shall to thy harp of solemn strain
No second place belong.

CADENCE

He fortunate whose eye
Could first thy beam espy,
Glimmering thro' shades of solitary night;
Whose hand, blest lyre, anew thy splendor could excite.
O heaths of Morven, and ye rocky isles,
That dare the surges of the western main,
Oft, when mild Eve diffused her rosy smiles
The master soothed you with his mighty strain:

Emergent from the chambers of the rain,
While airy shapes with rapture heard the lays,
As thro' the watry shore, and desert plain,
And shaggy caves obscure, in winding maze
The wondring echoes spread the accents of their praise.

Ode XV. The Vale of Woe
After the gaelic manner

Heard ye not the raven scream?
Saw ye not the sable stream?
Heard ye not the bleak wind blow
Adown the vale of woe?

In John Logan's *Poems* (London, 1781) appeared
a metrical version of Ossian's *Hymn to the Sun*,
which seems to merit quotation:

O Thou whose beams the sea-girt earth array,
King of the sky, and father of the day!
O sun! what fountain hid from human eyes,
Supplies thy circle round the radiant skies,
For ever burning, and for ever bright,
With heaven's pure fire, and everlasting light?
What awful beauty in thy face appears!
Immortal youth, beyond the power of years!

When gloomy darkness to thy reign resigns,
And from the gates of morn thy glory shines,
Thy conscious stars are put to sudden flight,
And all the planets hide their heads in night;
The queen of heaven forsakes the ethereal plain,
To sink inglorious in the western main.
The clouds refulgent deck thy golden throne,
High in the heavens, immortal and alone!
Who can abide the brightness of thy face!
Or who attend thee in thy rapid race!

The mountain oaks, like their own leaves decay;
Themselves the mountains wear away;
The boundless main that rolls from land to land,
Lessens at times, and leaves a waste of sand;
The silver moon, refulgent lamp of night,
Is lost in heaven, and emptied of her light;
But thou for ever shalt endure the same,
Thy light eternal, and unspent thy flame.

When tempests with their trains impend on high,
Darken the day, and load the labouring sky;
When heaven's wide convex glows with lightnings dire,
All ether flaming, and all earth on fire:
When loud and long the deep-mouthed thunder rolls,
And peals on peals redoubled rend the poles;
If from the opening clouds thy form appears,
Her wonted charm the face of nature wears;
Thy beauteous orb restores departed day,
Looks from the sky, and laughs the storm away.

The next important contribution to the Celtic-English poetry of the day was from the hand of John Walters, the Younger: [1] *Translated Specimens of Welsh Poetry in English Verse. With some Original Pieces, and Notes* (London, 1782).[2] There are three metrical versions of Welsh bardic poems from Evans's *Specimens*, apparently written under the influence of Gray.[3] The first of the "original

[1] Master of Ruthvin School; not to be confused with John Walters, the Elder, noted lexicographer and Rector of Landough.

[2] The Preface is dated 1780.

[3] Walters pays a tribute to Gray's poems based on material in Evans (see p. 35). Further evidence that Walters was making a study of Gray at the time is found in the announcement: "Shortly will be published a new edition of the *Translated Specimens of Welsh*

pieces," *Lewellin and his Bards*, deals with a bardic contest at the time of Edward I. The other, an *Ode to Cambria*, begins:

> Cambria, I love thy genius bold;
> Thy dreadful rites, and Druids old;
> Thy bards who struck the sounding strings,
> And wak'd the warlike souls of kings.

After continuing for forty-four lines with general praise of Cambria, it then turns to the glories of Welsh poetry:

> O'er my soul
> Such varied scenes in vision roll,
> Whether, O prince of bards, I see
> The fire of Greece reviv'd in thee,
> That like a deluge bursts away;
> Or Taliesin tune the lay;
> Or thou wild Merlin, with thy song
> Pour thy ungovern'd soul along;
> Or those perchance of later age
> More artful swell the measur'd rage,
> Sweet bards whose love-taught numbers suit
> Soft measures and the Lesbian lute.

The conclusion is a lament that all this greatness has now passed.

In 1783, Thomas F. Hill furnished a good anti-dote to the sentimentalism of Macpherson by contributing to the *Gentleman's Magazine* numerous translations of genuine Ossianic poems. The first of

---

Poetry in English Verse. To which will be added, translations of the Latin pieces of Mr. Gray." The announcement is in a pamphlet (1786) containing odes by J. W. the Younger and J. W. the Elder.

these, *Ossian agus an Clerich* (pp. 33–36) consists of forty-seven four-line stanzas. All of Hill's contributions were privately printed in 1785 under the title *Ancient Erse Poems.*[1]

The year 1784 was of unusual importance in the development of the Celtic Revival because it marked the publication of the first edition of a carefully prepared folio volume, now very rare, by Edward Jones. By quoting the long title in full, it is possible to give at least an idea of the material Jones had gathered: *Musical and Poetical Relicks of the Welsh Bards: Preserved by Tradition, and Authentic Manuscripts from Remote Antiquity; Never Before Published. To the Tunes are Added Variations for the Harp, Harpsichord, Violin, or Flute. With a Choice Collection of the Pennilion, Epigrammatic Stanzas, or, Native Pastoral Sonnets of Wales, with English Translations. Likewise a History of the Bards from the Earliest Period to the Present Time: and an Account of their Music, Poetry, and Musical Instruments, with a Delineation of the Latter. Dedicated, by Permission, to His Royal Highness the Prince of Wales. By Edward Jones, of Henblas, Llandderfel, Merionethshire* (London, 1784). The frontispiece is an engraving, from the drawing by

---

[1] For the other pieces see the *Gentleman's Magazine,* pp. 140 ff., 398 ff., 489 ff., 590 ff., and 662 ff. For the facts about the privately printed volume, see Nichols's *Literary Anecdotes,* VIII, p. 154; John Martin's *Bibliographical Catalogue of Privately Printed Books* (2d ed., 1854), p. 98; and Charles Vallency in *Archaeologia,* VII, pp. 276 ff.

Loutherbourg, of the Bard made famous in Gray's poem of that name. In addition to various quotations from Gray's poems from the Welsh, and the numerous items noted in the title, there is a fine poem by William Whitehead, *The Battle of Argoed Llwyfain*, elaborated from a few verses attributed to Taliesin.[1] At the beginning of the collection of *Pennilion* (pp. 30–39) is an essay on communal composition in Wales, including several pages of Welsh poetry with English translation in verse. The last section of the book (pp. 45–78) is devoted to Welsh music. It is significant that Jones's work aroused enough interest to justify the publication of a second edition, greatly enlarged, in 1794. Various other editions appeared, that of 1808 being so full of Welsh poetry with English translations as to be a representative summary of the best English poetry derived from genuine Welsh sources.

The next work to be considered is one which can hardly be taken seriously to-day, a narrative poem of twenty-five hundred lines by John Joshua Proby, first Earl of Carysfort: *The Revenge of Guendolen* (12 copies privately printed in 1785).[2] The author

---

[1] Subsequently reprinted on pp. 141 ff. of Bell's *Classical Arrangement of Fugitive Poetry* (London, 1791).

[2] The *D. N. B.*, following John Martin's *Privately Printed Books*, has erred in assigning a conjectural date of 1786, for a four page review of the poem appeared in the *European Magazine* for April, 1785, pp. 274 ff. Although the piece appeared anonymously at first, it was included in the Earl of Carysfort's *Dramatic and Narrative Poems* (London, 1810), II.

naïvely tells us that he "was led by the notes of the
last Canto of Mr. Hayley's Essay on Epic Poetry,
to try the effect of the northern mythology in a
poem of the narrative kind." [1] Carysfort seems to
have confused Celtic and Teutonic ideas in a more
fundamental and hopeless way than any of his
contemporaries. He knew of Pope's projected epic,
Brutus, in which there were to be Druidical elements; [2] he was steeped in the Norse poems of Gray
and had evidently read *The Bard;* he was familiar
with Mason's *Caractacus* or with some treatise on
Druidism; he wanted above all to fulfill Hayley's
request for a British epic. But he was not aware,
any more than Mason had been until Gray told him,
that "Woden himself is supposed not to have been
older than Julius Cæsar" and that "neither he nor
his Valhalla were heard of till many ages after." [3]
So Carysfort innocently attributed the Odinic system to the "Huns" who lived a few decades after
the fall of Troy. The Britons of the poem still cling
to the classical mythology, but apparently believe
in the rite of the rocking stone, supposed in the
eighteenth century to be Druidical.

The five endless books of *Guendolen* deal with
Locrine's desertion of his wife, Guendolen, for his

---

[1] Introduction, p. 4.

[2] For the facts about Pope's *Brutus*, see my article in *The Journal
of English and Germanic Philology*, XVIII, October, 1919, and the
references there given.

[3] See Gray's letter to Mason, January 13, 1758.

Scythian captive, Estrildis; Estrildis's vain attempt
to protect Guendolen by invoking various divinities;
Guendolen's revenge on Sabra, daughter of Locrine
and Estrildis; and finally Estrildis's death by suicide. Incidentally, the poem includes a paraphrase
of Gray's *Fatal Sisters*. There is also a striking similarity between Gray's lines at the end of *The Bard:*

> He spoke, and headlong from the mountain's height
> Deep in the roaring tide he plung'd to endless night.

and the last lines of *Guendolen:*

> "Now, Guendolen," she cried, "I scorn thy power,
> And all thy rage is vain. Oh welcome, death!
> No longer arm'd with terrors, thus I court thee."
> So saying, from the steep and lofty cliff
> Headlong she plung'd into the rolling flood.

The reviewer in the *European Magazine*, stigma-
tized the anonymous poem as "evidently . . . the
adventurous essay of a youth ambitious to try his
strength on the bow of Apollo," and again as "the
work of a youth of fortune" — hard words for a
man well on towards forty!

During the winter of 1785–1786, attention was
again called to *Ossian* by the production of a play,
Werther, adapted from Goethe. Like the original,
it contains a reading from *Ossian* at its emotional
climax.[1]

---

[1] In the three-act version of the play published at London in 1802
this occurs in Act II. According to Genest, *Werther* was first produced at Bath, December 3, 1785, and subsequently at London,
Bristol, and Dublin.

Included in *Poems on Several Occasions, By the late Edward Lovibond, Esq.* (London, 1785) [1] are two Celtic pieces. The opening lines of the *Imitation from Ossian's Poems* run thus:

> Brown Autumn nods upon the mountain's head,
>   The dark mist gathers; howling winds assail
> The blighted desert; on its mineral bed
>   Dark rolls the river through the sullen vale.
>   On the hill's dejected scene
>   The blasted ash alone is seen,
>   That marks the grave where Connal sleeps;
>   Gather'd into mould'ring heaps
>   From the whirlwind's giddy round,
>   Its leaves bestrew the hallowed ground.
> Across the musing hunter's lonesome way
> Flit melancholy ghosts, that chill the dawn of day.

Lovibond's other Celtic poem, *The Complaint of Cambria,* contains several good lines, with phrases taken from Gray's *Bard.* After the opening stanza (which chides "Miss K— P—" for singing English verses instead of Welsh), the poem continues:

> Revere thy Cambria's flowing tongue!
> Tho' high-born Hoel's lips are dumb;
> Cadwallo's harp no more is strung,
> And silence sits on soft Lluellyn's tomb:
>   Yet songs of British bards remain
>   That, wedded to thy vocal strain,
> Would swell melodious on the mountain-breeze,
> And roll on Milford's wave to distant echoing seas.
>
> O sing thy fires in genuine strains!
> When Rome's resistless arm prevail'd,

---

[1] Lovibond had died in 1775.

When Edward delug'd all my plains,*
And all the music of my mountains failed;
  When all her flames Rebellion spread,
  Firmly they stood — O sing the dead!
The theme majestic to thy lyre belongs,
To Picton's lofty walls, and Cambrian virgins['] songs.

In 1786 appeared a volume almost comparable in importance to Edward Jones's *Musical and Poetical Relicks of the Welsh Bards*, the title, *Historical Memoirs of the Irish Bards*, showing that the author, Joseph Cooper Walker, was trying to do for the Bards of Ireland what Jones had already done for those of Wales. It is a book of some two hundred pages large quarto, compiled with great care. The authors quoted, historians, musicians, and poets, represent the best scholarship of the day. Frequent comments on *Ossian* show clearly that Walker realized the extent to which the Celtic material had been tampered with by Macpherson. It is to be regretted that in the Appendix of a hundred and twenty-four pages he could not find room for the translation of Evans's *Dissertatio de Bardis* which Walker says was "undertaken at my request, and executed with elegance and spirit by my Brother Samuel Walker." Nevertheless, the work is interesting and full of information. Of the Irish poems translated into English verse, nearly all are by Carolan, who died in 1738. On the whole, Walker's

* Edward I put to death all the Welch Bards. [Lovibond's note.]

Memoirs did more to arouse interest in Irish music and literature than to propagate them.

In 1787 Edmund Baron de Harold, already known as a successful translator of *Ossian* into German, published some *Poems of Ossian Lately Discovered* (Düsseldorf), in which the title page, Preface, and almost the whole book give the impression that these are genuine Gaelic poems written long ago by Ossian and now first translated. But the "Preface to My Country" (not to be confused with the regular Preface) freely acknowledges that all the pieces are de Harold's own composition. The author is not, accordingly, to be classed with Macpherson, Clark, and Smith. The "translation" is in prose, but not the "measured" prose of Macpherson. Some interest attaches to the cleverness of the plots, but there is, on the whole, little literary merit.

In marked contrast to the pseudo-Celtic lamentations which Macpherson had connected with the name of Ossian, came the *Antient Gaelic Poems respecting the Race of the Fians, collected in the Highlands of Scotland in the Year 1784* (Dublin, 1787) by Mathew Young, D.D., M.R.I.A. In 1786, Young read a sound and interesting paper before the Royal Irish Academy, and subsequently published it, together with a number of Gaelic poems and their translations into English prose. He justly criticizes Macpherson for the liberties he took with his material, but praises Mr. Thomas F. Hill and the printer, Mr. Gillies "to whom the Erse language is, on many accounts, much indebted." The Gaelic poems published by Young are: *Ossian's Courtship of Evirallin; The Lamentation of the Wife of Dargo; The Combat of Con, Son of Dargo, and Gaul, Son of Morne; The Combat of Osgar and Illan, Son of the King of Spain; The Invasion of Ireland by Erragon; The Prayer of Ossian;* and *The Death of Oscar.* While Young was not poet enough to put these pieces into English verse, his work showed a wholesome tendency to find out what Gaelic poetry really was.

In the same year John Ogilvie called attention in the Advertisement of his *Fane of the Druids* to the fact that "It is somewhat extraordinary, that a theme so fruitful of the wild and the wonderful, as is that of Druidism, should not have arrested imagination, so as to have become, at an early period, the subject of a poem. Yet, though Druidical rites are described in epic poetry, and Druidical actors have figured in the drama, no poetical performance, either ancient or modern, has (so far as the author knows) the ritual ceremonies and observances of this celebrated order of men, professedly as its subject." [1] Accordingly under the protection of anonymity, Ogilvie proceeded to give the public *The Fane of the Druids*, a rather remarkable poem of

[1] Page vii.

fifty pages, large quarto, devoted exclusively to Druidism. The profuse notes show that he had made a thorough study of the classical historians, and his leisurely heroic couplets set forth most of the obtainable facts, tinged here and there with a touch of poetic idealization. From a poem of such length quotation would be useless, but a convenient summary is given by the Argument:

Introduction. Manners, habitations, etc., etc., of the first inhabitants of North Britain. Face of the country. Mansion of the Druid, and account of his person, dress, and character. Assembly of the Druidical order. Speech of the Arch-Druid. Building, and consecration of the Fane. Signal of approbation from heaven. Ceremony of lopping the mistletoe. Sacrifice. General feast. Office of the chief Druid in the Fane. Office of the Bardi, and subjects of their songs. Sublime ideas of the Deity. Oblation of the Warriour. Office of the Euvates, and of the sacred Virgins. Ceremony, time, and manner of gathering the Mistletoe, and honours paid to him who brought it. Wonderful fable of the serpent's egg. Druidical tenets and principles. Astronomical discoveries. Doctrine of the Metempsichosis [*sic*], and application of it to promote the practice of virtue. Of the mundane dissolution, and renovation. Moral lessons. Effect on character and practice. Manner of receiving young warriors after conquest. Peace and general felicity. Comparison of their manners with those of modern times. Conclusion.

In view of the increasing public interest in the subject, one is not surprised to find that two years later
the author, "encouraged by the favorable reception" of his poem, added thirty-eight pages more,
large quarto, in the form of *The Fane of the Druids.
A Poem. Book the Second* (London, 1789). In
commenting on the first book, the critic of the
Monthly Review said justly:

The particulars which are preserved concerning the
Druids, are well suited, both from their nature, and
from the obscurity which time has thrown over them,
to furnish a theme for poetical description. The writer
has happily seized the idea of exhibiting, in the dress
of poetry, the tenets, rites and customs, of this ancient
race, as far as any vestiges of them remain. The description is wrought up in the form of an interesting
tale; the writer has thrown over the narrative a lively
colouring of fancy, and has expressed his conceptions
in easy and harmonious verse. In his notes he has collected the principal facts respecting his subject, and
discussed several doubtful points, with much ingenuity.

Again our attention is called to an anonymous
poem, an *Address to Loch Lomond* (London),[1] which
gave unstinted praise to Ossian's harp, and added
in a note a few ill-chosen words on the Ossianic controversy:

[1] No date, but the Catalogue of the British Museum supplies 1788.

Along these streams, and on that rising flood,
The plaintive sound of Ossian's harp was heard,*
Its numbers lofty, genuine from the heart,
The praise of heroes sung, and beauty's charms,
Which e'en the savage breast can charm. Its notes
Of woe wild-warbling still methinks I hear.
The King of Morven from his airy hall
Bending looks down upon his hills of mist.
A thousand forms of heroes wait the chief,
Musing on scenes and feats of other years.
   Wrapt in the mist that veils yon mountain's brow,
Descend ye hov'ring spirits, and inspire
Of Britons old the independent soul. . . . [Pp. 18–19.]

Now that *Fingal* had been put into English verse
so many times, the Rev. Edward Davies, "Lecturer
of Sodbury," felt called on to rescue *Temora* from
"the dislike English readers in general feel for measured prose." [1] Accordingly he included a metrical
version of the first book of *Temora* in his *Vacunalia:
consisting of essays in verse, on various subjects, with
some translations* (London, 1788). As a fair specimen of his work I quote, from pages 195–196, Fingal's lament over Oscar:

And art thou fall'n, O lovely beam of light!
O Oscar, Oscar, arm of Fingal's might!
The heart of Selma's chief, the King of years,
Beats o'er thy wounds, and Fingal melts in tears.

* Much has been said on the question, whether the Poems of
Ossian be genuine; but from the evidence that appears in favor of the
affirmative, when duly considered, one might, it would seem, with
equal propriety call in question the existence of the Gaelic language,
as doubt of their authenticity. [Page 25.]
   [1] *Vacunalia*, p. 167.

Thy coming wars, thy distant deeds I see,
Thy future fame — but ah! no fame for thee!
Here dost thou stop, ere half thy course is past,
And thy first day of glory is thy last.
But when shall joy return to Selma's halls?
When, grief depart from Morven's tow'ry walls?

A great deal more of *Temora* was subsequently put
into English verse of about the same quality,
probably by Davies,[1] but it was never printed—perhaps because the public, in spite of Davies's statement to the contrary, really preferred the measured
prose of Macpherson.

In 1788 four different publications printed posthumously William Collins's *Ode on the Popular
Superstitions of the Highlands of Scotland; Considered as the Subject of Poetry; Inscribed to Mr.
John Home.*[2] It is, briefly, an exhortation to poets
in general, and to Home in particular, to use in their
verse whatever untouched material they could find

---

[1] In the copy of *Vacunalia* at the Library in Cardiff I find seventy-
four MS. pages, unsigned, of *Temora* in English verse. At the end
of the MS. is the following unsigned note: "The foregoing fragments
in MS. having been hastily versified were laid by with an intention of
correcting them. As I have no access at present to the works of
Ossian, I transcribed the papers without alteration merely to pre-
serve them to a future opportunity."

[2] Collins died in 1759, at the very beginning of the Celtic Revival.
The Ode was recovered long after his death and first printed, so far
as I can discover, in 1788. See the *Transactions of the Royal Society
of Edinburgh*, I; *Scots Magazine*, 1788, pp. 195-199; *European Magazine*, 1788, pp. 241 ff.; *Annual Register*, 1788.

in the Highlands — whether folk tales, ancient bardic songs, or native traditions.

During the last three years of this decade a writer using the bardic name "Owain o Feirion" contributed to the *Gentleman's Magazine* numerous English prose translations of Welsh poems; of these at least one, *The Battle of Gwenystrad*, was immediately put into verse by W. Williams.[1] Apparently Welsh poetry was becoming more and more of a fad, for the same magazine was glad to print another poem, by another Williams, said to be one of the two "regular bards" in the world. But the explanatory letter is too delightful to omit:

The pieces you herewith receive were written by Edward Williams, of Flimstone, near Cowbridge. He is absolutely self-taught, and was never at school. . . . His first productions were in the Welsh language. About the age of twenty he was admitted a *Bard* in the ancient manner; a custom still retained in Glamorgan, but, I believe, in no other part of Wales. . . . Besides Edward Williams, there is, I believe, now remaining only one regular Bard in Glamorgan, or in the world; this is the Reverend Mr. *Edward Evans*, of Aberdale, a Dissenting Minister. . . .

Edward Williams is now about forty years of age, and lives by the humble occupation of *a journeyman*

[1] See the *Gentleman's Magazine*, 1790, pp. 214, 354, and 451. For the other pieces, see *ibid.*, 1788, p. 821, *The Graves of the Warriors of Britain;* 1789, pp. 335–336, *The Battle of the Vale of Garant;* 1790, pp. 989–990, *Cynvelyn's Incantation.*

mason. He is remarkably sober and temperate, very seldom drinks any strong liquors, and if he sometimes tastes them, it is in very small quantities, and [he] was never seen in liquor.

After this introduction to the public, it is not strange that Edward Williams found himself able to break into print almost at will.[1]

A really good poem, important for its Scandinavian, and to some extent for its Celtic mythology, appeared in 1789 — Richard Hole's *Arthur; or, The Northern Enchantment. A Poetical Romance, in Seven Books*. Hole's metrical version of *Fingal* (1772) had brought him some poetical reputation, and now on the publication of *Arthur* he found himself the recipient of high praise both in prose and verse.[2] Like Gray, Hole was interested in both Scandinavian and Celtic religious rites; in the former he was well read, but for the latter he seems to have drawn largely on Geoffrey of Monmouth and James Macpherson — truly a remarkable

[1] The letter quoted is from the *Gentleman's Magazine*, 1789, pp. 976–977; for various poems by Edward Williams, see *ibid.*, 1789, pp. 1036–1037; 1792, pp. 956–957 (cf. *Scots Magazine*, 1792, p. 303); *Walker's Hibernian Magazine*, pp. 182–183.

[2] See the *Ode, On Reading Mr. Hole's Arthur, or the Northern Enchantment*, in Hugh Downman's *Poems* (2d ed., 1790), pp. 195 ff.; the reprint of over 400 lines of *Arthur* in the *Annual Register* for 1790, pp. 148 ff.; and the review in the *European Magazine*, March, 1790, for a summary and favorable comment. A full summary with critical analysis is available in Professor F. E. Farley's *Scandinavian Influences in the English Romantic Movement*, pp. 109–115.

combination. His indebtedness to *Ossian,* as well as his doubt of the antiquity of that work, is explained at length in the Preface. The Scandinavian part of the poem was apparently written with more confidence than the Celtic, and its pictures stand out more vividly. While the poem is too long to be treated here in detail, it may be said that the plot hinges on the contest between Arthur and Hengist for the rule of Britain and for the love of Inogen, daughter of Merlin. The Celtic hero, supported by Merlin, is finally victorious, and the poem ends with the reconciliation of Arthur and Inogen.

In the same year Charlotte Brooke, whose knowledge of the Irish language had already stood her in good stead,[1] published one of the most important collections of Celtic-English poetry which appeared in the late eighteenth century: *Reliques of Irish Poetry: consisting of heroic poems, odes, elegies, and songs, translated into English verse: with notes explanatory and historical: and the originals in the Irish character. To which is subjoined An Irish Tale. By Miss Brooke* (Dublin, 1789). As indicated by this title, Miss Brooke's *Reliques* contains some sixteen Irish poems, for all of which she gives translations into English verse. Some of the pieces are early, some by so late a writer as Carolan; all of them have considerable merit. While Miss Brooke's

[1] She had contributed a translation in verse of Carolan's *Monody on the death of Mary Maguire* to Walker's *Historical Memoirs of the Irish Bards.* See *Brookiana,* II, by C. H. W. (London, 1804).

ability as translator was obviously greater than as versifier, nevertheless her work is as good as that of many who were attempting the same sort of thing.

In its day the *Reliques of Irish Poetry* was widely read and favorably noticed. Of particular value were the introductions and notes to the various poems and the essay entitled *Thoughts on Irish Song*. It is noteworthy that, though several of the poems deal with Oisin, this Oisin is the genuine saga hero — not the sentimentalized Ossian of Macpherson.

At the end of the book the author gives a composition of her own called *Mäon: an Irish Tale*, for which she says in the brief Advertisement: "The story of the following Tale is to be found in the ancient history of Ireland, and is related by Keating, O'Halloran, Warner, etc." After reading the one hundred and ninety-five stanzas of *Mäon*, one feels that Miss Brooke might better have limited herself to the work of translating. This one original contribution has no merit except in the few bardic songs, from the best of which the following stanza is quoted:

> Mäon! bright and deathless name!
> Heir of Glory! — son of fame!
> Hear, O hear the Muse's strain!
> Hear the mourning Bard complain! —
> Hear him, while his anguish flows
> O'er thy bleeding country's woes.
> Hear, by him, her Genius speak!
> Hear her, aid and pity seek. [Page 350.]

A good deal more poetic merit attaches to the stirring poem by "H. S." freely rendered from the first piece in Evans's *Specimens*. The editors of the *European Magazine* thought it worthy of two pages in their issue of October, 1790,[1] but present limitations of space allow me to quote only the opening lines:

HIRLAS: A Poem
By Owen, Prince of Powis
From Evans's *Specimens of Welsh Poetry*

Fair rose the morn in splendor dress'd,
The ruddy Sun illum'd the East,
The clang of armour fill'd the air,
Th' impetuous warriors rush'd to war.
Sword clash'd with sword; the slippery plain
Was strewed with Saxon heroes slain.

In William Sotheby's blank verse account of his *Tour through Parts of South and North Wales* (1790) is a good deal that may be termed Celtic-English poetry. Of special interest is the description of the invasion of the Island of Mona,[2] with the author's debt to Mason's *Caractacus* duly acknowledged in the following note:

This is a faint attempt to imitate the masterly description of the invasion of Mona, by Tacitus. The admirers of *Caractacus* will recollect, towards the conclusion of that drama, an imitation of the above passage, equally spirited as judicious.

[1] Pages 308–309.
[2] Pages 37–39 in the editions of 1790 and 1794.

Apparently Sotheby was already gathering material to be used in his Druidical drama, *The Cambrian Hero*, which he published some ten years later.[1]

In Frank Sayers's well-known volume, *Dramatic Sketches of Northern Mythology* (London, 1790) there is very extensive use of Celtic material. *Moina, A Tragedy* is the story of a Celtic heroine who has been carried off by a Saxon, Harold. Her lover, Carril, disguises himself as a bard and finds her in Harold's castle, but fails to effect her delivery. Harold conveniently dies, but the Saxons insist on burying Moina with him; at this juncture Carril, in somewhat Ossianic style, dies of a broken heart. Around this slender thread of plot there is, however, a great deal of good verse replete with references to Celtic and Scandinavian mythology. In these lyrics the reviewer of the *European Magazine* found "an originality, a vigour, and a grace, certainly not surpassed by Macpherson, by Chatterton, or by Gray."[2]

More distinctly Celtic, and more inherently dramatic, is Sayers's tragedy *Starno*, included in the same volume. In the Introduction he says:

[1] See below, p. 178.

[2] See the *European Magazine*, April, 1793, pp. 268 ff. In 1807 appeared the fourth edition, with a good essay on Druidism accompanying *Starno*, and in addition a *War-Song of Fingal, from the Gaelic* (pp. 236 ff.), of which Sayers says: "This song was translated *literally* from the Gaelic by a native of the Scotch Highlands, and was given, in prose, to the author of this work."

The story of the following Tragedy, like that of the foregoing, is fictitious, but I hope not entirely inconsistent with the manners and customs of the Celtic people. As the scene of action is laid in Britain, I have been obliged to desert the mythology of the Saxons for the institutions and ceremonies of the druids; some of these ceremonies have already been received by the public with delight, as displayed in the admirable tragedy of Caractacus; but although the variety and magnificence of the Gothic religion is by no means rivalled by the Celtic, yet there appeared to me some parts of it untouched, which might be introduced into dramatic poetry with tolerable effect.

From the first act of *Starno* I quote a brief specimen:

CHORUS

Hail, Hesus, hail!
By thee inspir'd,
The mailed warrior dauntless braves
The singing spear and biting blade —
Hail, Hesus, hail!
I see thee climb
Thy scythed car,
And drive the furious steeds
Amid the falling foe.
Who dares to meet thine eyes of flame?
Who dares to brave thy falchion's edge,
The thunder-bolt of war?
Death hovers round thy stately crest
And poized spear,
While terror rises in the blast,
And sails before thy car.

Raise aloft, Andate, raise
Thy golden shield —

Loudly strike its echoing brim,
And wake the sound of victory —
From the purple field it comes
To pierce our holy groves —
Rude it rushes thro' the shade,
The roaring rocks return
The joyful noise;
The warrior hears — he shouts aloud,
And clangs his massy arms.

STARNO

Ye venerable men, nor songs of triumph,
Nor fond endearments of a long-lost child,
Force from my shuddering mind the bloody vow
These hallow'd groves have heard — the noblest captive
Is solemnly devoted to the god —

DAURA

The noblest captive?

DRUID

Yes, lady, the god demands his right,
Our pray'rs were heard — he rais'd his arm of conquest.

DAURA

My fearful soul beholds the gathering woe
That hastes to overwhelm me. Father, father,
Why dost thou cast thy mournful eyes on Kelric?
Is he the noblest captive? — doomed to death?
Away! who dares to touch a princely guest?
Who dares to touch that Kelric who restor'd
His long-lost daughter to her father's arms?
That Kelric who, entic'd by Daura's words,
Has quitted all for her?

CHORUS

Fair lady, peace,
Hesus demands the blood we vow'd to him.

James Mylne wrote two decidedly Celtic dramas,
both published posthumously [1] in his *Poems, Consisting of Miscellaneous Pieces, and two Tragedies*
(Edinburgh, 1790). In the first of these, *The British
Kings*, the characters are: Cadwallan, King of
ritain; an old Druid; and Arthur, Prince of the
Britons. The piece does not compare favorably
with Mason's *Caractacus*, and I have not found any
evidence that it was ever performed. *Darthula*, on
the other hand, is of some literary merit; it was, of
course, derived from Macpherson's Ossianic poem
of the same name, but Mylne, though he calls the
piece a tragedy, takes the liberty of preserving the
lives of both Darthula and Nathos. In the history
of the Celtic Revival this play is of special importance because, in spite of Macpherson's influence,
it is genuine saga material, handed down through
the ages under the name of *Deirdriu*.[2]

[1] Mylne died in 1788.

[2] The Deirdriu story had been published in English in Dermod
O'Connor's translation of Keating's *History of Ireland* (London,
1723), pp. 175–181. Macpherson had Darthula (i.e., Deirdriu) killed
by an arrow, but remarked in a note that according to tradition she
"killed herself on the body of her beloved Nathos." In one of the
standard early Irish versions of the story (as printed by Windisch
in his *Irische Texte*) Deirdriu flings herself out of a chariot and strikes
her head against a rock in order to escape her captors. For various
versions of the story, see the references given in Douglas Hyde's
Literary History of Ireland, pp. 302 ff., and Windisch, *Irische Texte*,
pp. 59 ff.

MINOR SYMPTOMS OF INTEREST IN THE
CELTS, 1781-1790

The writers of Celtic-English poetry were so prolific during the years 1781–1790 that it is necessary to include in this brief résumé several items which properly merit treatment in greater detail.

1781. A group of friends who "were wont to assemble for the purpose of friendly converse at the King's Arms Tavern, in Poland St.," London, constituted themselves the Grand Lodge of the Order of Druids, a society organized "to promote good fellowship, hilarity, and brotherly love." Numerous subsidiary lodges were established, and by the end of the century the order was a friendly society of some importance. A general (though unscholarly) interest in Druidism was taken by its members, and many poems and essays were published.[1]

William Warrington's *History of Wales* (3d ed., 1781) contains an excellent account of the bards, and a poetical translation by John Walters, the Younger, of a poem by Llywarch Hen.

An English prose translation of David ap Gwilym's *Cwydd to Morvydd* was printed in the *Gentleman's Magazine* for October, page 483.

1782. An English metrical version of Mirvin Goch's fragment, *The Praise of Hurlech,* of which the

---

[1] See *The Druids' Magazine,* 1st series, II, pp. 25 ff.; also the *Encyclopædia Britannica,* VIII, p. 598 and XI, p. 219.

prose had appeared in Craddock's *Letters from Snowdon* (1770, p. 59), was printed in the *Gentleman's Magazine* for January.

In the first stanza of *The Muse; or Poetical Enthusiasm* by John Scott, the Quaker poet, Ossian's voice is said to be as sweet as Shakespeare's.

A Sonnet, Translated from the Original Irish by Edward Nolan appeared in the *European Magazine* for August, page 100; cf. December, page 471.

W. J. Mickle published anonymously *The Prophecy of Queen Emma*, a clever skit on the poems attributed to Ossian and to Rowley.

Maria Cosway exhibited a picture entitled *Darthula. A Scene from Ossian*.[1]

William Hayley showed a great interest in Celtic poetry in Books III and V, *passim*, of his poetical *Essay on Epic Poetry: in five epistles to the Rev. Mr. Mason*, and made special mention of Mason's *Caractacus* on page 113.

1783. James Barry's picture showing Ossian, was exhibited in this year. (See above, p. 110, n. 2.)

The Rev. Edward Davies published *Aphtharte or the Genius of Britain, a Poem*, reviewing the list of Celtic heroes who fought for liberty — Caractacus, Arviragus, Arthur, etc.

1784. Edward Ledwich read a paper before the

[1] See *Richard Cosway, R. A. and his Wife and Pupils*, by George C. Williamson (London, 1897), p. 17. The picture was the object of some humorous lines by Peter Pinder in his *More Lyric Odes to the Royal Academicians* (London, 1785), pp. 21–22.

Society of Antiquaries of London (published in 1785) protesting against sentimental idealization of the Druids, and insisting that they were superstitious savages. (See *Archaeologia*, VII, pp. 303 ff.)

1785. Dr. John Campbell's metrical translation of the *Fragment of an Ode by Taliessin* appeared in the *European Magazine* for May, page 382.

On pages 607–608 of the *Scots Magazine* appeared a twenty-nine stanza poem (copied from the *London Chronicle*) which purports to be from an old Welsh story "in the manner of Ossian." The author of this worthless production, *Llewyn and Gyneth*, was a Mrs. Robinson.

An Ossianic piece was included in Sir Egerton Brydges's volume, *Sonnets and Other Poems; with a versification of The Six Bards of Ossian.*

1786. *Malvina. A Tragedy*, perhaps by John Reddel, was privately printed.[1]

In the *European Magazine* for March appeared an elegiac poem of eight stanzas *On Cambria* by Peter Pindar (Dr. John Woolcot).[2]

1787. The *Poems* of John Macgilvray, published

---

[1] On p. 101 of John Martin's *Bibliographical Catalogue of Privately Printed Books* (2d ed., 1854) is the following entry: "Malvina. A Tragedy. Glasgow: Printed for Andrew Foulis. 1786. 8vo. pp. 65. A MS. note in Mr. Maidment's copy states that the author was Mr. John Reddel, surgeon, Glasgow." I have not been able to find a copy in the Catalogue of the British Museum *s.v. Reddel, Malvina*, or *Ossian*.

[2] For the facts of the composition of the poem, see the *European Magazine*, October, 1791, p. 303.

in this year, were not wholly detached from the Celtic Revival. See pages 61 and 68.

The Rev. Luke Booker spoke favorably of "Ossian's Muse of Fire" in his poem *The Highlander*, page 31.[1]

A poem entitled *The British Kings*, mentioning Caractacus, Andraste's grove, and Druids, was published in the *Gentleman's Magazine* for January and February.

1788. A short romance in verse, *A Vision: in which is Introduced A Tale of Other Times*, by "Alcander," appeared on pages 124–127 of the *European Magazine* for August. The tradition of a massacre of the Welsh bards by Edward I, about which Gray wrote his poem *The Bard*, forms the basis of one of the incidents.

Since W. J. Mickle died in 1788, we may mention here his poem *May-day; or, The Druidical Festival*, first published in 1806.[2]

1789. On January 10, Sylvester O'Halloran read before the Royal Irish Academy an Irish poem, *The Ode of Goll, the Son of Morna*, with an English

[1] Although the poem is not dated, the fact that it was published in 1787 appears on page 36 of Booker's *Miscellaneous Poems* (Stourbridge, 1790), where *The Highlander* is reprinted.

[2] In the Rev. John Sim's edition of *The Poetical Works of William Julius Mickle* (London, 1806). Though Mickle's reconstruction, largely imaginative, of the Druidical rites on May-day would doubtless have astonished the Druids themselves, the poem has many beautiful lines.

translation. These were printed in the *Transactions of the R. I. A.*, for 1788, II, part 3, pages 7 ff.

1789. On pages 383–384 of the *European Magazine* for November was printed a song in honor of Caractacus, signed "Strotha," said to have been "sung in the Caractacan Society."

Owen Jones and William Owen Pughe published the *Barddoniaeth Dafydd ab Gwilym.* There are no translations of the poems, but the scholarly Introduction and Appendix are in English.

On pages 497–498 of the *Gentleman's Magazine* for June appeared an English prose translation by Gillies [1] of a Gaelic poem called a *Chronicle of the Kings of Scotland.*

An *Ode on the Birthday of His Royal Highness The Prince of Wales, August 12, 1789,* signed with the initial "A," was printed in the *Gentleman's Magazine* for August, pages 143–144. The second and third stanzas contain Welsh matter of some interest.

In the same magazine for September, page 839, appeared an anonymous *Sonnet to a Welch Harper.*

1790. The Bard, a Sonnet from the Antient British, by W. H. Reid, was published in the *Gentleman's Magazine* for May, page 450.

---

[1] This was probably not the Reverend John Gillies, D.D., nor yet the Royal Historiographer of that name, but rather John Gillies the bookseller of Perth, who published a volume of Gaelic poems entitled *Sean Dain*, etc. (Perth, 1786).

A short *Passage in Ossian Versified* was included in the *Works* of Soame Jenyns, pages 201–202.

As one looks back over the decade from 1781 to 1790, it is evident that the Celtic-English poetry produced amounted to more, in both quality and quantity, than that of the previous twenty years. The excellent judgment shown in compiling and translating by Walters, Jones, Walker, Pinkerton, and Charlotte Brooke added to our literature an amazing amount of English poetry from Celtic sources of unquestionable authenticity; while the original work of Mathias, Ogilvie, Hole, and Sayers reflected, in poetry of even greater intrinsic merit, the spirit of the early Celts.

CHAPTER VIII

1791-1800

THE last decade of the century opened with the publication of several Celtic poems in the *Miscellaneous Works* of Andrew M'Donald, *alias* Matthew Bramble. *Minvela, a Fragment, Imitated from the Gaelick,* consists of eighteen Spenserian stanzas of unusual poetic beauty, with marked influence from *Ossian.* There is, however, very little action, and the author's method is too leisurely to make any short quotation representative. While the long romance, *Velina,* extends to ninety-nine stanzas of the same form, it likewise is incomplete. From the varied spelling of the proper names (e. g., *Gaur* and *Gaul, Cathmor* and *Cathmoor*) it appears that the poem had never received its finishing touches. The plot deals with the love of Arvan for Velina, the cruelty of her guardian Farquhard, who is called "a revengeful chief," the capture of both lovers by Gaur, and various shameful plans from which the heroine is rescued in a manner suggestive of the Gothic romance. In passing it may be noted that the same volume contains a parody of Gray's *Bard.*

In 1791 George Richards produced his *Aboriginal Britons, a Prize Poem, Spoken in the Theatre at Ox-*

ford, of which two editions were issued in that year.[1]
This brilliant eulogy of the ancient Celts received
many favorable criticisms, Lord Byron's being the
most noteworthy, for the poem was one of the few
to receive genuine praise in *English Bards and Scotch
Reviewers:*

> Where Richards wakes a genuine poet's fires,
> And modern Britons glory in their sires.

The Argument, as prefixed to the second edition, is
as follows:

> Address to the first Navigators of the South-Seas —
> Wild state of the country — contrasted with Italy as
> improved by culture — Aboriginal Britons considered
> as individuals — the Man — the Woman — Consid-
> ered as to their national character — Their domestic
> state — promiscuous concubinage — ignorance of other
> countries — description of a day in time of peace, in-
> cluding circumstances of their domestic œconomy —
> Their wars — fondness for war — internal dissentions
> and their consequences — manner of fighting — be-
> haviour after a defeat — treatment of captives after a
> victory — Religion — the objects, which give rise to
> natural religion — Druid Grove — Magic rites, and hu-
> man sacrifices — Bards — Doctrines — transmigration
> and immortality of the soul and its effects — Charac-
> teristics of Liberty in the savage state of this island
> — its extinction in the early stages of our Monarchy

---

[1] A long extract is in the *Annual Register* for 1791, pp. 141 ff.

— its revival and influence in the present civilized state of manners, as producing public security, giving rise to public works, and calling forth the powers of the mind.

As the notes to the poem show, Richards was thoroughly familiar with the works of the Celtic antiquaries and with Mason's dramatic poem, *Caractacus*.

Elated by his success, Richards hastened to publish the *Songs of the Aboriginal Bards of Britain* (Oxford, 1792).[1] The collection contains but two "songs," *The Battle* and *The Captivity of Caractacus*. In the first of these Richards borrowed so directly from Gray's *Bard* that he had to insert a note calling attention to the fact that he had slightly changed Gray's imagery and mode of application. Both poems show a combination of poetic power and accurate information almost worthy of Gray, as a short quotation may suggest:

> The Bards perceiv'd the yielding throng,
> And quick resum'd their magic song:
> By your fathers' warrior-shades;
> By antique Mona's holy glades;
> By Cambria's rocks, that streamed of yore
> With many a Conqueror-Roman's gore;
> By each car and flaming brand,
> That drove bold Julius from our strand;
> Turn: — and blushing fear to fly;
> Revere your kind, and dare to die.

[1] A long extract is in the *Annual Register* for 1792, pp. 175 ff.

The soul shall quit the stiffening clay,
    And mount through air to brighter spheres;
In warlike sports with Hesus play,
    While Hoel's music charms the ears.
                        The Battle, pp. 8–9.

In 1792 there appeared at Bath two volumes entitled *Poems, Chiefly by Gentlemen of Devonshire and Cornwall*, edited by Richard Polwhele. Among the contents are *Ossian Departing to his Fathers*,[1] *Imitated from Macpherson's Ossian, 1780*, by the editor, another Ossianic poem by Richard Hole, and a significant *Elegy on Gray* by "N." In the same year Polwhele printed in *Walker's Hibernian Magazine*[2] an ode called *Mona*, of which the reader will doubtless find one stanza enough:

"Shroud, in the billow mist's deep bosom, shroud
    My ravag'd isle!" — the voice was vain —
Mona! mark yon kindling cloud
    That seems to fire the main;
As, flashing to the distant skies,
Broad the hostile flames arise
From the reverential wood;
Red its central gloom with blood!
Many a white rob'd Druid hoar
Totters in the stream of gore —
Meets the faulchion's furious blow,
Sinking, execrates the foe;
Or, across the *Cromlech's* stone,

[1] Reprinted in Polwhele's *Poems* (1806), II, pp. 216 ff.
[2] For October, p. 176; reprinted in Polwhele's *Poems* (1806), III, pp. 7–9.

Pours his dark mysterious moan;
Or, grasps his shrine, and hails the stroke,
Stabb'd beneath his holy oak;
Yelling, while the maniac maid
Hurries down the dimwood glade;
And uproots her bristling hair,
Paler amid the ghastly glare!

A very important contribution to the literature of the Celtic Revival was the publication of *The Heroic Elegies and Other Pieces of Llywarc Hen, Prince of the Cumbrian Britons: with a Literal Translation*, by William Owen [Pughe] (London, 1792). The work contains a long and interesting introduction on the history of bardism and the life of Llywarc Hen, followed by the poems, with Welsh and English in parallel columns. As the translation is excellent and the notes are scholarly, it is not to be wondered that the literary magazines reviewed it favorably. Especially enthusiastic was the *Monthly Review:*

At length a spirit of investigation seems to have arisen in Wales, which promises to throw much light on the antiquities of this principality, and to clear up many an obscure point of early British history: may no littleness of national vanity, no *order-spirit*, betray any of the learned inquirers into statements tending to magnify the knowledge, to embellish the tenets, or to throw back the antiquity, of our "old bards, the famous Druids." . . .

Mr. Owen gives a most pleasing picture of the religion of the Druids, which, he says, is no more inimical
to christianity than the patriarchal theism of Noah
and of Abraham. He attributes it to a severe and in-
flexible morality. Its doctrine of the transmigration
of souls has been held by many christians. . . . [Here
follows a long quotation from one of the elegies.] May
the author speedily favour us with the works of Taliesin[1]
and the whole series of British bards! . . .

The *Critical Review* was likewise loud in its praises,
though both magazines objected to the "unmusical"
arrangement of Pughe's English.

By a strange coincidence, while the *Monthly Review* was expressing its regret that these translations
from the Welsh had not been made in a style like
"that of Ossian's editor, which is remarkably convenient for rendering with elegance the complex
epithets of rude poetry," an American named
Richard Alsop was engaged in transmuting *Ossian*
from its measured prose into four-line stanzas of
very doubtful merit. In *American Poems, Selected
and Original* (1792),[2] appeared his translation of the
fifth book of *Temora*, beginning thus:

[1] It seems that Pughe's translations of Taliesin, announced at this
time, were never published as a separate work. His material was
probably included in the *Myvyrian Archæology* (1801), of which he
was an editor.

[2] The copy in the Harvard Library has no date on the title page,
but the Preface is dated "Litchfield (Connecticut) June 1793." For
the reference to Alsop, I am indebted to Professor F. E. Farley.

The hosts like two black ridges stood,
  On either side wild Lubar's stream;
Here Foldath frown'd a darken'd cloud,
  There Fillan shone a brightening beam.

Their long spears glittering in the wave,
  Each hero pour'd his voice afar;
Gaul struck the shield, the signal gave,
  At once both armies plung'd in war.

In February and March of 1794 the *European Magazine* featured some metrical versions of *Ossian* signed by the initials "G. N." That the early eighteenth-century fondness for the closed heroic couplet still survived, appears from this specimen of *Ossian's Apostrophe to the Sun*:

Vast orb of fire! refulgent as the shield
That guards the warrior on th' embattled field,
Say, bright subduer of the cheerless night,
Whence are thy beams and everlasting light?
Thou comest forth, thou lift'st thy awful head,
And all the multitude of stars are fled:
Pale hangs the moon, yet ling'ring o'er her grave;
And sinks, unnoticed, in the western wave.
But thou thyself (for who can match thy powers?)
In solitary splendor lead'st the hours.

Neither in the remaining thirty lines of this poem, nor in *The Song of Colma*, do we find any unusual poetic charm.

The tone of Edward Williams's critical remarks in his *Poems, Lyric and Pastoral* [1] seems to mark a new

---

[1] London, 1794, 2 vols.

step in the development of early English romantic poetry. First had come an attempt to revive the mythology of the Celts and of the Scandinavians; next, a prolonged effort to distinguish between the customs and rites of these two peoples, so sadly confused by the early poets; [1] and at length there came to be a real rivalry between the two mythologies for use in English poetry, with Edward Williams an avowed champion of the Celts. In the *Advertisement* to his *Ode on the Mythology of the Ancient British Bards*, he wrote:

How truly ridiculous to an Ancient British Mythologist, appears the BARD of GRAY with its *savage Scandinavian Mythology;* the same may be said of other English poems, that, except in this particular, possess the highest poetical excellence.

I cannot help thinking that the *British Bardic* Mythology would supply Poetry with many new ideas, and much of very pleasing imagery; it seems to me far more *rational, sublime, and congenial to Human Nature*, than the *superlatively barbarous* and *bloody Theology* of the EDDA, which *some depraved* imaginations are so charmed with.

Throughout the two volumes of his *Poems*, Edward Williams strove to put into practice the theory he had expressed so strongly. Being a thorough master of both Welsh and English, and having

---

[1] See above, pp. 9 ff.

in addition some slight knack of handling English forms of verse, he translated from Welsh poetry into English poetry without any deadening intermediate step. What Evan Evans translated into English and Latin prose, Gray and others had put into poetry which represented the spirit of the original only in a reflected light; but what Williams took from the Welsh, he reproduced with a direct simplicity. As a result, his translations both in quantity and in fidelity to the originals are among the most important of the Celtic Revival, while his original poems "in the Welsh manner" are by no means negligible. It must be understood, however, that though his ideas may have been "rational, sublime, and congenial to Human Nature," he never produced a poetic masterpiece in English.

A little prose pamphlet of fifty-eight pages published at this time probably helped to crystallize the available information on Druidism — *Antiqua Restaurata. A Concise Historical Account of the Ancient Druids* (London, 1794), by Jacob des Moulins. Although modern scholars would find it too dogmatic and definite on many uncertain matters, it furnished the poets of that day with what they wanted —a convenient list of the Celtic gods, and a concise statement of what were (in the opinion of des Moulins) the principal Druidical doctrines. As this is one of the few treatises in which anyone has had the temerity to attempt a definition of these doctrines, it may prove worth while to enumerate them here.

I. None must be instructed but in the sacred groves.

II. Mistletoe must be gathered on the sixth day of the month, if possible, and cropped with a golden bill or pruning hook.

III. Every thing derives its origin from Heaven.

IV. The Deity is one, and infinite, and consequently to confine his worship within walls, is inconsistent with his attributes.

V. The arcana of the sciences must be committed to the memory, but not to writing.

VI. The powder of the mistletoe makes women fruitful, and is a panacea in medicine.

VII. The disobedient are to be excluded from the sacrifices.

VIII. Souls are immortal, and after death transmigrate into other bodies.

IX. The world is eternal, *a parte ante*, and shall never be destroyed, unless by fire and water.

X. On extraordinary emergencies, a man may be slain, and future events predicted from the manner in which the body falls, or moves after it has fallen, as well as from the manner in which the blood flows, or the wound opens.

XI. Malefactors or prisoners, and in case of neither, innocent persons are to be slain upon the altar, or burnt alive inclosed in a wicker Colossus, in honour of the Gods.

XII. All commerce with strangers must be prohibited.

XIII. He that comes last to the assembly of the states, ought to be put to death.

XIV. Children are to be educated apart from their parents, and never to be admitted publicly into their company, till they are fourteen years of age.

XV. Money lent in this world will be repaid in the next.

XVI. There is another world, and they who kill themselves, to accompany their friends thither, will live with them there.

XVII. Letters given to dying persons, or thrown on the funeral piles of the dead, will be delivered faithfully in the other world.

XVIII. The moon is a sovereign remedy for all diseases.

XIX. The disobedient are to be excommunicated, deprived of the benefit of the law, avoided, and rendered incapable of any employ.

XX. All masters of families have a power of life and death over their wives, children, and slaves.

Among the more unusual developments of the Ossianic poems was *A War Song. From the Ancient British*,[1] which adopted Macpherson's Gaelic heroes

---

[1] By "R. C." Published in the *European Magazine*, July, 1796, pp. 52–53.

for convenience, but had them defeated by the Cumbrian Britons. The poem opens thus:

> Arno! strike the lyre again,
>   To arms! the furious Morcar cries;
> What means yon tumult on the plain,
>   Come, let the sons of Cumbria rise.

Shortly before the end of the century the Rev. William Tasker, author of the *Ode to the Warlike Genius of Great Britain*,[1] published *Arviragus*, *A Tragedy*.[2] In spite of the statement in the *Monthly Review* that "This is a curious tragedy, without either plot or poetry," the play was read more widely than would have been possible with such limitations. The action is as follows: Arviragus, King of Britain and son of Cymbeline, is besieged at Winchester by the Romans under Lucius. Dishonorable terms of surrender are rejected by the Britons, who sally forth and successfully attack the Roman camp. A Roman maiden, Marcella, is carried captive into Winchester, and the forces of Lucius are depleted. While negotiations are being carried on for peace on terms which give Arviragus the Roman Emperor's daughter as his wife, two of the Britons kill each other in jealous rage over their fair captive, Marcella. The play, though called a

---

[1] See above, p. 127.

[2] The Preface is dated August 24, 1796; a second edition appeared in 1797, and several passages were reprinted in *Poems on Military and Naval Subjects* (Bath, 1799 [?]).

tragedy, ends happily with the marriage of Arviragus to the Emperor's daughter, and with the arrival
of Horatius, Marcella's Roman lover. In addition
to a short lyric by the Bard "Clewellin," there is a
martial song in Act II, and a nuptial song in Act V.

MARTIAL SONG BY CLEWELLIN
If to the battle ye shall go,
Rush impetuous on the foe;
Rush on the foe without dismay,
Like roaring lions on their prey:
Or wolves, that from the mountain's rock,
Descend upon the fleecy flock. . . . [Page 39.]

NUPTIAL SONG BY CLEWELLIN
O Sun! exulting in thy radiant sphere!
And thou, fair sister! milder Luna! hear!
And both propitious deign to shine
On the brave son of Cymbeline. . . . [Page 53.]

Although I cannot find much merit in these verses,
— or in any others which substitute exclamation
points for emotional appeal,— the play is significant
from the historical standpoint. Among the authorities cited are: Geoffrey of Monmouth, Tacitus,
Juvenal, Cæsar, and Lucan.

Still another metrical arrangement of *Ossian* appeared before the end of the century — George
Goodwin's Paraphrase on the Latter Part of the
Eighth Book of Ossian's Temora.[1] It is peculiar
only in the verse form, which begins in blank verse
and then changes to stanzas of this type:

[1] In the *European Magazine* for February, 1798, p. 114.

Ossian, lo! the spear of Fingal
Radiant glistens in thy hand,
'T is not as the staff of infants,
Strewing thistles o'er the land.[1]

Perhaps the most astonishing result of Gray's influence on the Celtic Revival was the production in 1798 of James Boaden's historical play *Cambro-Britons*.[2] The general subject is the invasion of Wales by Edward I, which alone would be enough to make us suspect that the author's inspiration had come from Gray. But this is not all; Act III, scene 5, of *Cambro-Britons* is from beginning to end simply a dramatization of *The Bard*, with the omission of the long prophecy. And as Genest justly remarks, this is the best scene in the play.

CAMBRO-BRITONS, ACT III, SCENE 5

(*The scene changes to a narrow pass, along which the King's army must march. A rough and angry torrent bounds it in front, overhung by inaccessible crags. The drum of the invading army is heard and louder as they approach. At the moment when the King attended enters upon the stage, with a hideous yell, the Bards rush to the verge of the cliffs, and with haggard forms, seen only by the glare of the torches they carry, like furies pour out their execrations on his head, in a full chorus to the harp only.*)

[1] Practically the whole poem is quoted, with unbounded praise, in S. J. Pratt's *Gleanings in England*, of which various editions appeared at the end of the century.

[2] Published at London in 1798. Genest, in his *History of the English Stage*, says that it was acted twelve times, the first performance being on July 21 at the Theatre Royal, Haymarket.

CHORUS

Ruin seize thee, ruthless King!
Havock choak thy furious way!
Desolation's raven wing
Sweep thee from the eye of day!
Ruin seize thee, ruthless King.
Ruin seize thee, ruthless King.

HEREFORD

Say, what are these? — The spirits of the mountain
Yelling amid the storm!

MORTIMER

Despair sustain me! —
To arms!

HEREFORD

Behold, my lord! from forth the band
One rushes on — and, by the sudden silence,
Prepares to speak. Th' undaunted king advances!

FIRST BARD

Edward, I call thee! if thou dar'st, then hear me.
Would I could add the eagle's piercing scream,
And all the savage sounds that awe the desert,
To thunder on thee — tyrant, persecutor —
Cool, unrelenting, bloody ravager! —
Behold the last remains of that high race
Thy policy has butchered! . . . .

[*The first bard continues this execration for 22 lines more, interrupted only by the chorus — "Ruin seize thee, ruthless King."*]

KING EDWARD

I 'll bear no longer! To your arms, my friends!
Let not these haggard wretches thus dismay ye!
Silence the race forever!

(*Charge sounded. — The soldiers rush out. — The Bards, all but the principal one, fly. — The woods are seen to take fire in the distance.*)

FIRST BARD

That I laugh at.
He who dares die is master of the means.
My fate is plac'd beyond thee. Think not, king,
The generous stream that beats here shall embathe
A ruffian's falchion. — I hear the groans
Of my dear dying friends! — Their parting breath
Shrieks curses on thee! — May it fall like mist,
And deadly vapours poison all around thee! —
Hark! the last feeble wail! — and now all 's silent.
See, where their thin shades flit among the clouds! —
Behold! They beckon me! and thus I join them. —

(He flings himself into the torrent below him, and with the sound of trumpets the scene drops.)

Another drama strongly influenced by Gray's *Bard* was destined to appear within a short time — William Sotheby's *Cambrian Hero, or Llywelyn the Great*.[1] This is an historical tragedy based on the conflict between Edward I and Llywelyn the Great for the sovereignty of Wales. Of considerable literary interest is Llywelyn's consultation with the Sibyl and the spirits of the dead Druids. By a strange coincidence Sotheby took the idea of the scene from *Macbeth* and the wording of the Druids' song from *The Bard*.

LLYWELYN

I do remember, in a low arched cave,
Upon this mountain's brow old Sibyl lived;
Versed it is said in Merlin's prescient lore.
Her I 'll consult. . . .

---

[1] The volume is not dated, but it appeared *ca.* 1800.

Sibyl (*sitting under the arch of her cave*)
I knew thou'dst come —
Thy *horoscope*, what e'er belongs to thee
In Fate's recorded page, was read last night.
Thy star consulted 'midst a thousand spells.
And for to aid me in my magic art
I called the spirits up, of Llowarch Hen,
Of Mychdeirn Beirdd — Cian — and Talhaiarn —
Those holy druids — high Heaven's first-born priests —
They — who are waiting in King Arthur's court —
And for a thousand years have been confined
In a dark cave — i' th' bowels of the earth —
Them did I call — and now thy fate is fixed —
That if with courage thou pursuest the war,
Thou shalt through London's streets triumphant ride —
Thy brows encircled with a diadem. —
Llywelyn — hark — th' attesting voice of heaven.

[*Amid much thunder and lightning, Llywelyn, deceived, like Macbeth, by the ambiguous words of the Sibyl, decides to continue his course. Then four Druids sing a song drawn largely from Gray's Bard, of which the last lines are these*]:

Llywelyn rouse, and strike the blow,
Let ruin seize th' invading foe;
Then glory on thy banners wait,
Recording Fame thy deeds relate.

Some mention must be made here of Richard Llwyd (Bard of Snowdon) although his most important work, *Poems, Tales, Odes, Sonnets, Translations from the British*, etc., did not appear until 1804. In 1800 he published a poem so profusely annotated that on some pages there is only a single line of verse — *Beaumaris Bay, a Poem: with Notes* . . . ; *Particulars of the Druids*, etc. While the present study is not concerned with the poetical account of a trip around Beaumaris Bay, the Bard of Snowdon included so much information about Welsh literature in the notes that they are by no means negligible. Of special importance are the numerous Welsh poems with English translations.

So many incidental references to the Druids have been passed over silently in these pages that it seems only fair to quote a sample in which the imagery is vivid and poetic. These lines from Dr. Darwin's *Address to the Swilcar Oak* [1] would hardly have been understood by the average reader in 1750, but by 1800 Druidism was so much a matter of common knowledge that they adorn without obscuring the body of the poem:

> Erst, when the Druid bards, with silver hair,
> Pour'd round thy trunk the melody of prayer;
> When chiefs and heroes joined the kneeling throng,
> And choral virgins trill'd the adoring song;
> While harps responsive rung amid the glade,
> And holy echoes thrill'd thy vaulted shade. . . .

MINOR SYMPTOMS OF INTEREST IN THE CELTS, 1791–1800

1791. Oscar and Malvina, a "ballet pantomime," was produced at Covent Garden on October 20, 1791, and on May 22, 1797. The Argument shows an interesting plot, which, unlike most Ossianic

[1] From the *European Magazine*, March, 1800, p. 226.

pieces, ends happily. It was printed in 1791, and by 1792 there were four editions. The operetta was also produced at Hamburg in 1795 and another edition there printed.

Under his bardic name of Dafydd ddu Feddyo, David Samwell published his English verse translation of one of Dafydd ap Gwilym's poems, in the *Gentleman's Magazine* for January. The next month's issue contains his *Ode for the First of March, 1791, St. David's Day. Inscribed to the Gwyneddigion Society of London.* This is a general panegyric upon Welsh history, literature, and life.

1792. Throughout the year various literary magazines published English bardic poems by Edward Williams.[1]

In *Comàla, a Dramatic Poem, from Ossian, As performed at the Hanover-Square Rooms, on Thursday 26th January, 1792, set to music by Miss Harriet Wainright* (London [1792]), Miss Wainright has achieved a sort of dramatic poem in three acts, by excerpting long passages from Macpherson's *Ossian* and adding appropriate stage directions.

A translation of Macpherson's *Lathmon* into Latin hexameters had been completed as early as 1765 (possibly 1762) by Robert Trevor, Viscount of Hampden. This was subsequently published in folio, sumptuously bound, by John Trevor (Parmae,

---

[1] See the *Gentleman's Magazine*, pp. 956–957; *Scots Magazine*, p. 303; *Walker's Hibernian Magazine*, pp. 182–183.

1792), the title of the volume being *Britannia,
Lathmon, Villa Bromhamensis.*

1793. The Rev. Richard Warner cited *Ossian* as
an historical source in support of his own theory of
burial among the ancient Celts;[1] and the *European
Magazine* said in perfectly good faith, "Those who
have doubted the authenticity of Mr. Macpherson's
translations, will find very strong reasons in these
volumes to abandon their infidelity." Thus by a
circular type of logic Warner's theories were supported by Macpherson, and Macpherson was vindi-
cated by Warner! In Warner's second volume is
included a poem, *Hengistbury Head*, containing
(p. 208) one reference to the Druids.

In his poem, *The Ruins of a Temple*, Joseph Jefferson wrote,

> 'T was his a Thor and Woden to withstand
> While Druid temples trembl'd all around,[2]

as if Woden and Thor had been gods of the Druids,
and further obscured the matter in an ambiguous
note. Apparently he did not distinguish between
Norse and Celtic.

On pages 9–11 of Samuel Thomson's *Poems* (Bel-
fast, 1793) is an Ossianic imitation entitled *Colmal,
an Eclogue, in Imitation of Ossian.* Colmal here
laments the death of her lover, Norval, who has been

---

[1] See his *Topographical Remarks, relating to the South Western Parts
of Hampshire,* I, p. 66.

[2] London, 1793, p. 3.

slain by the men of Lochlin. Coleridge referred to *Ossian* in the Preface of his 1793 volume. (Cited by Professor Beers.)

In the *Ode on Erecting an Academy of Inverness*, the "lays sublime of [the] hoary Bard of war" were mentioned, and a hope was expressed that a "future Ossian" would arise.[1]

1794. A second edition of Edward Jones's *Musical and Poetical Relicks of the Welsh Bards* (see above, p. 136) was published with many additions.

A pastoral poem published in the *Gentleman's Magazine*, page 843, has some Celtic elements; the setting is the bank of the River Clwyd, and the characters are Nest and Morven.

1795. A descriptive account in blank verse, of the old Serpentine Temple of the Druids at Avebury in North Wiltshire, by Charles Lucas, proved to be of more antiquarian than poetic value. As the Preface to the second edition (1801) stated, "an attempt at poetry was the last thing the author intended." Lucas appears to have been writing under the influence of Stukeley.

On page 950 of the *Gentleman's Magazine* appeared an anonymous rendering into Greek verse of twenty-eight lines from Macpherson's *Death of Cuthullin*.

John Jones (Glanygors), Thomas Roberts, and the Rev. J. S. Jones combined to establish another

---

[1] Anonymous. *European Magazine*, April, 1793, p. 311.

Welsh literary society — the Cymreigyddion. It met (according to the *Transactions of the Cymmrodorion Society*, 1909–1910, p. 69) at the Golden Fleece on Queen St.

1796. The *Gentleman's Magazine* printed in January an Ode by William Boscawen containing twenty lines on the influence of the ancient British Bards and their power of inspiring warriors in battle.

The *Cambrian Register* for 1795 (published in 1796) contains a translation into English verse by Evan Evans of several stanzas of Welsh poetry, as well as a quantity of information interesting to students of Welsh literature.

Anna Seward's descriptive and reflective poem, *Llangollan Vale*, is of special interest here because of the frequent references to Welsh history and literature.[1]

William Gilbert's poem, *A Solitary Effusion*,[2] begins with a description of the aged stream that heard the war-song of the ancient Britons under Caractacus,

> and has lived to hear
> That song again from centuries of Death
> On Mason's lyre revived. [Page 42.]

Then follows a description of a Druid grove.

---

[1] Later appeared two excellent versifications by Miss Seward of passages in *Ossian* — *Crugal's Ghost*, and *The Ghost of Cuchullin*; see her *Poetical Works* (Edinburgh, 1810), III, pp. 15 ff. and 21.

[2] Published, along with his *Hurricane*, in 1796.

Abraham Portal's *Vortimer; or the True Patriot*
is an unimportant tragedy published in 1796, though
we learn on page 4 that it "was written long ago."
The chief *dramatis personae* are Vortigern, Vortimer,
Cartigern, Hengist, Horsa, Baldread, Locrinus,
Ambrosius, Rowena, and Locrina. Apparently the
play was never acted.

Richard Polwhele's *Sketches in Verse* (London,
1796) contains three Ossianic poems: *To Colma* (p.
78), *Oscar* (p. 79), and again *To Colma* (p. 80).[1]

1797. Thomas Gisborne wrote at some length
about Bards and Druids and quoted from Mason's
Caractacus in his *Elegy to the Memory of the Rev.
William Mason*, published at London.

George-Monck Berkeley committed the old
blunder of confusing Norse and Celtic mythology.[2]
In his *Maids of Morven* he consigned both Oscar and
Malvina to "Odin's hall."

1798. W. L. Bowles made a similar mistake in his
St. Michael's Mount.[3]

In the Supplement to the *Gentleman's Magazine*
for 1798 appeared Edward Dupre's short poem in
heroic couplets, *On Rear-Admiral Lord Nelson's Victory.* This song of victory begins its praise of British
prowess with an apostrophe to the painted chief-

---

[1] For observations on one of Polwhele's later poems derived in part
from *Ossian* and in part from Bürger's *Lenore*, see my short article
in *Modern Language Notes*, XXIX (May, 1914), pp. 157–159.

[2] See above, p. 11.

[3] Cited in Professor Farley's *Scandinavian Influences*, p. 150.

tains who withstood Cæsar. The piece is significant only as showing how instinctively writers were coming to associate the idea of national independence with the history of the Celts.

An American author signing only the initials "C. C." produced some heroic couplets of no little beauty entitled "Ossian's Address to the Moon," which were printed in *The Weekly Magazine* (Philadelphia).[1]

1799. In Volume I of his *History of the Anglo-Saxons*, Sharon Turner devoted one whole chapter and parts of two others to a discussion of the British Bards. His ideas were in the main sound, and his enthusiasm was justified. Although most of his facts were derived from such excellent authorities as William Owen Pughe, Evan Evans, Edward Williams, and Edward Jones, he was severely criticized by Pinkerton (Preface to *Babour*), by the *Critical Review* (January, 1800), and by Malcolm Lang (in a note to the *Dissertation on Ossian's Poems*). To these and other doubting Thomases he replied in his *Vindication of the Ancient British Poems of Aneurin, Taliesin, Llywarch Hen, and Merdhin, with Specimens of the Poems* (London, 1803).

The Rev. Luke Booker had already disappointed many of his readers by including no definitely Celtic material in his poem *The Highlander*, which, in spite

---

[1] Part II, 1798, pp. 220–221. They had originally appeared in the *Merchants' Daily Advertiser*, but in a slightly different form.

of its attractive title, proved to be devoted to the economic and domestic hardships encountered in Scotland. But in a nameless production entitled *A Sequel-Poem to The Hop Garden* (Newport, 1799) he digressed at length on the rites of the Druids (pp. 84–85).

In this year Dr. John Leyden wrote his *Ode on Scottish Scenery and Manners* (for the date see his *Poems*, 1858, p. 291, note), but I have no evidence that it was published during the eighteenth century.

The *Cambrian Register for 1796* (Vol. II), published in 1799, contains a Welsh poem translated into English prose and another into English verse (pp. 554–566).

William Belsham, in his *Essay on Epic Poetry*, was one of the few adverse critics to parody the style of *Ossian:*

Of this strange jargon, may it not be said in the style and language peculiar to this poet — Thy thoughts are dark, O Fingal! thy thoughts are dark and troubled. They are as a dim meteor that hovers round the marshy lake. Comest thou, son of night, in the darkness of thy pride, as a spirit speaking through a cloud of night? Thou art enveloped in obscurity, chief of Morna! like the moon veiled in a thick cloud. Thy words are dark like songs of old, son of the cloudy Morven! (*Essays*, II, pp. 442–444.) [1]

---

[1] Not having had access to a copy of the first edition, I cannot with certainty assign a date prior to 1799.

1800. The sixth stanza of the anonymous *Dirge of Belgium*, on page 257 of the *Gentleman's Magazine*, contains Druidical material with specific mention of the goddess Andraste.

Among the *Poems* of Anne Bannerman (Edinburgh, 1800) is a sonnet (p. 96) based on *Ossian*, while her sequence of *Sonnets from Werther* is introduced by a passage from *Ossian* which had already been quoted in *Werther* and in *The Letters of Charlotte*.

On page 161 of the *Gentleman's Magazine* is a translation by "Peris" into English verse of a Welsh poem in honor of Bardsey. The original is said to have been written about 1480 by Hywel ap David.

This last decade of the eighteenth century shows the Celtic Revival in full swing. *Ossian* had fallen off a trifle in popularity, perhaps, but the mythology of the Celts had come to be understood and appreciated. Constructive literary criticism had played a useful part in bringing to light the obscure beauties of Gray's *Bard*, and it was generally felt that Nathan Drake's words could safely be accepted with but slight reservation; regretting that more of Pindar's work was not extant, he said:

As it is, no piece can now be selected from his [Pindar's] works that can justly come into competition with the *Bard* of GRAY; over this inimitable ode a tinge so wildly awful, so gloomily terrific is thrown, as without any exception to place it at the head of lyric poetry.[1]

His opinion may also be taken as representative of the best critical judgment of the period when he pointed out that

> . . . the dreadful rites of Druidism, and the noble imagery of Ossian, afford valuable material for the lyric bard; the choruses of Mason, the songs of Richards, and some of the Sketches of Sayers are masterly specimens of what they can effect.[2]

[1] *Literary Hours* (2d ed., 1800), II, pp. 74–75.
[2] *Ibid.*, p. 96. For details of Drake's estimate of *Ossian*, see his essay *On the Superstitions of the Highlands of Scotland* in the same volume, pp. 207–258.

CHAPTER IX

Conclusion

I

SPECIAL ASPECTS OF THE CELTIC REVIVAL

IN the preceding chapters it has been necessary to eliminate from detailed consideration several important aspects of the Celtic Revival which it is only reasonable to mention in brief before bringing this study to an end. A vital consideration, which I have passed over with little comment, is the complex interrelation of politics and literature. The political relations between England and Ireland, always tense yet always changing, have played so important a part in the history of English literature that it has been out of the question to treat them in detail here. The same may be said of the political relations between England and Scotland, and, with some modification, of the relations between England and Wales. Every change in party was likely to be accompanied by a redistribution of government pensions, with corresponding bursts of enthusiasm and of bitter recrimination. I have elsewhere collected and commented on some of the most striking English satires against the Irish, Scots, and Welsh;[1] but no one, I think, has ventured to explain in detail the varying political motives which colored the criticism in all the literary magazines and influenced the reception of any particular poem by the public.

Another aspect of the Celtic Revival worthy of special consideration is the connection between religion and the study of primitive poetry. Every reader is familiar with the general fact that theologians of the eighteenth century were peculiarly attracted by anything that seemed to throw light on the state of primitive man as he came, supposedly, fresh from the hands of his Creator. Although Celtic poetry was by no means unique in making this appeal, some interest would have attached to pointing out the extent to which its study was promoted by religion.

A third special consideration, and one which I hope may be treated in the near future, is that of Celtic influences in American poetry. There was not, I believe, in America any such sudden outburst of the Celtic spirit as there was in England; the movement was less rapid and less brilliant. Nevertheless, we are all aware of various traces of Celtic mythology in American poetry of the nineteenth century, and of the persistent influence of *Ossian* on

[1] "The Wild Irish: A Study of some English Satires against the Irish, Scots, and Welsh," in *Modern Philology*, April, 1920, vol. xvii, pp. 147–185.

writers like Poe and Whitman. As a sample of the American interest, one of my correspondents, Professor Farley, has sent me a list of some sixteen scattering items, dating from 1786 to 1836, all from the Harris Collection of American Poetry in the Brown University Library.

A final matter of some importance, as to which the reader will be able to supply the necessary connecting links for himself, is the harmony of spirit among all the eighteenth-century poets and antiquaries who were seeking for information about the mythology of northern peoples. Gray's Celtic and Norse researches were related to each other in a most apparent way, as were those of Bishop Percy. The correspondence of these men with each other, and with Celtic and Norse scholars throughout Great Britain; the enthusiastic efforts of the Edinburgh group headed by Hugh Blair — all these were but a part of a general movement to enlarge the scope of poetry. If I have treated the Celtic Revival as an isolated phenomenon, I have done so because only by isolation is an intensive analysis made possible.

REV. W. MASON.

II

SUMMARY

In considering any literary movement a special interest always attaches to the work of the pioneers, and I have accordingly devoted a good deal of space to Morris, Evans, Gray, Mason, and Macpherson. These five men had different talents and supplemented one another in a peculiar way. Morris was the first and perhaps the best-informed of the group, but he did not live on into the period when English poets could draw directly on his great supply of Celtic lore. Evans came into prominence, accordingly, as a sort of medium to transmit in his *Specimens* a portion of the bardic wisdom of his deceased master. Gray was the poetical genius of the group, fifty years ahead of other great English poets in his feeling for the romantic spirit, which he caught in his Celtic and Norse productions as surely as Chaucer caught the spirit of the Renaissance. Mason, now remembered chiefly as the biographer of Gray, was the first to show the extent to which Celtic history and mythology could be used with success in dramatic poetry. Macpherson, the most daring, most influential, and least honorable of them all, swept across Europe on his waxen wings, only to fall into well-deserved obscurity.

Yet, attractive as a study of pioneers may be, it is

only through the study of a host of minor writers —
followers, and often mere imitators — that one can
come to estimate the interest taken by the general
public. It is to the amateurish efforts in the poetry
columns of magazines, to the reviews, and even to
the correspondence, that one must turn to compre-
hend the gradually increasing interest which the
public took in Celtic-English poetry. Gray's *Bard*
had very few admirers when it was first published,
for the simple reason that practically nobody knew
who the Bards were, or what their political influence
had been in the long struggle between England and
Wales; but before the end of the century the poem
was praised and quoted to an extent that baffles belief. And in the nineteenth century Longfellow
could actually explain the appearance of moss-
covered pines and hemlocks by likening them to
"Druids of eld with voices sad and prophetic" and
to "harpers hoar with beards that rest on their
bosoms"! By the time the Romantic Movement
was well under way, Celtic-English poetry was commonly written and universally understood. Its history in the nineteenth century could be followed to
show a fairly steady popularity in all its genuine
phases, until with the coming of still another new
century we find a new outburst — again with a
striking political connection — in the productions
of Lady Gregory, Yeats, Synge, Fiona Macleod, and
many others. But, as Evan Evans said when he

found himself getting into deep water, "Hæc a proposito nostro aliena sunt."

To the question, what was the contribution of the Celtic Revival to romanticism, one must reply with caution to readers whose opinions perhaps differ on the much mooted question, *What is romanticism?* Yet there is a general agreement that the poetry of the late neo-classical period suffered from lack of appeal to the imagination, from monotony of subject matter, from failure to describe adequately the grandeur of nature, and from over-use of the mythology of Greece and Rome. Such being the case, the Celtic Revival, along with many other contemporary tendencies, satisfied a certain desire for novelty. More specifically, since the glorious contrasts of mountain and ocean in Wales and Scotland and Ireland offered scenes of rare poetic beauty, it helped stimulate a new poetic interest in real nature as distinguished from conventional pastoral artificiality. Further, in spite of the obscurity in which Druidism always has been (and to some extent always must be) hidden, there emerged many brilliant images — now an awe-inspiring group of white-robed priests offering human sacrifice, now a chorus of Bards chanting potent curses against a Roman or British tyrant, now a valiant Celtic hero, dying, usually in vain, in the eternal struggle for liberty.

Although the very mass of this Celtic-English poetry is a valuable indication of the universal eagerness for new subjects, new settings, new moods, and even new forms of verse, one receives something of a shock on realizing that of all the poems considered in the preceding pages less than half a dozen might appear in an anthology of the best English poetry. The fact remains, however, and must be admitted freely if we are to grasp the literary significance of the Celtic Revival. Indeed, the fact is helpful in emphasizing the extent to which the late eighteenth century was a period of transition, of preparation for the brilliant era that followed. Except for the *Lyrical Ballads* and the work of Burns, the period from 1760 to 1800 is peculiarly destitute of poems that are in themselves masterpieces. It is, however, correspondingly rich in poems that show a reaching out into the unknown for something new, a striving for effects never before achieved. For the careful student of literary tendencies, it holds the record of a series of experiments for the most part only half successful, yet in their bearing on the history of literature perhaps as important as the brilliantly successful achievements of the years immediately following.

INDEX OF AUTHORS AND TITLES

INDEX OF AUTHORS AND TITLES